DAR

BE

DA

To my dear parents

to whom I owe everything. May Hashem bless them with fullness of years till one-hundred-and-twenty. And may they see nachas from all their children and grandchildren.

'Lamanatzeach' — To the chief musician: upon [the rising of] the morning star (*ayeles haShachar*), a psalm of David. My G-d, My G-d, why have You forsaken me? [Why are You] so far from saving me, from the words of my roar?

Psalms 22:1

Immediately before the rise of the morning star, the night is at its darkest. . . .
(Midrash Shocher Tov)

Shachar, 'morning' or 'dawn,' is related to *shachor,* 'black,' because the moment immediately preceding the dawn is the blackest, darkest part of the night.
(The Vilna Gaon, Avnei Eliyahu)

DARKNESS BEFORE DAWN

The Holocaust, And Growth Through Suffering

by
Rabbi Ezriel Tauber

adapted by
Yaakov Astor

ISBN 1-878999-11-7 Hardcover
ISBN 1-878999-12-5 Softcover

Shalheves
P.O. Box 361
Monsey, N.Y. 10952
(914) 356-3515

Wholesale Distribution:
Feldheim Publishers
New York, Jerusalem

". . . her flashes are like the flashes of fire, the flame of G-d (Shalheves Kah)."
(Shir HaShirim 8:6)

CONTENTS

CHAPTER 4

CHAPTER 5

CHAPTER 6

CHAPTER 7

APPENDIX

PREFACE

Odeh Hashem meod b'fi u'b'soch rabim a'halaleno, "I will thank *Hashem* for the overabundance with my mouth; and in the midst of the public, I will praise Him." (*Tehillim* 109:30)

IF ONE IS GUSHING LIKE A FOUNTAIN with an overabundance of thanks to *Hashem*, what can he possibly do, where can he possibly go to express even a portion of that thanks? David HaMelech answers, ". . . in the midst of the public, I will praise Him." He must go public with his expression of thanks and praise.

With this understanding, I publish this book, which has been bubbling inside of me for a long time, waiting to burst forth. As a survivor of the Holocaust, publication of material related to that experience is profoundly emotional. My emotions spill over with thanks to *Hashem* for the extraordinary insights into the meaning of life and suffering the experience has furnished me.

Although the substance of this book springs from my life experience, this is not an autobiography (though I will include a few personal experiences in this introduction). This book it is about my discovery of meaning in the very suffering and tragedy which was the Holocaust. My primary intention is not just to present a unique understanding of the suffering inflicted by the Nazis, but to help others discover meaning in the personal holocaust he or she may be suffering.

I am aware that to write such a book is presumptuous. Still, this effort is not based on my own imaginings, but on teachings of Torah which cover the topic of suffering and predate not only the Holocaust but all other episodes of Jewish torment. Even when one possesses the principles of Torah outlook, the task of explaining them clearly and tactfully is extremely difficult. Nevertheless, the difficulty — and perhaps even the impossibility of the task — do not free us from attempting to explain, in a Torah context, the nature of Jewish suffering, including that endured at the hands of the Nazis.

In truth, I have been hesitant and filled with great reservations about the publication of this book because I know that I am truly unworthy of such a vital and monumental task. Nevertheless, I am compelled to go against my strong reservations because whenever I have related these insights in public, I could see the positive impact on peoples' faces. I feel that *Hashem* has given me unique and valuable insights into the subject for one reason: to pass them on to others. By holding back and not passing them on, I believe that I will violate *u'b'soch rabim a'halaleno*, ". . . in the midst of the public, I will praise Him."

Of course, a question still needs to be addressed: If the message is so important and true, how is it that no one else ever put the material together in this fashion? I have asked myself this question thousands of times. I have even heard it from others, including great scholars, educators, and yeshiva principals. (Ultimately, the truth of my presentations was not questioned; rather puzzlement was expressed as to why this material was never presented in this way before.) Who am I to bring forth this material? I have the same question. I, too, am baffled.

One answer could be as follows: If this same book had been written by a world-renowned Torah personality, you may have been likely to accept the material not necessarily on its own merit, but because a great person wrote it.

Chazal teach, "Who is the wise man? He who learns from all men."[1] The Maharal of Prague explains that if a person learns wisdom only from a great person, then he never knows whether the wisdom was a means or an end. In other words, he never knows if the wisdom was a way to make contact with a great person (a natural desire in all of us), or if it was the wisdom itself which attracted him. However, when one accepts wisdom from any person, even someone whose stature is far below that of his own, clearly wisdom itself was the goal. Consequently, one is "the wise man."

Historically, we acquired wisdom largely through our access to eminent people. However, we, of the modern day, who are being prepared to receive *Moshiach,* are an orphaned generation. We do not have the opportunity to develop our entire *hashkafa* (Torah outlook) via a closeness to the undisputed leaders of the generation. Even though these leaders exist, day-by-day and minute-by-minute guidance from them is not possible given our great need and their general inaccessibility. And thus, we are indeed orphaned.

However, "Wisdom will be publicized on the street,"[2] Shlomo HaMelech said in reference to our days, the End of Days. Torah will be on every street corner. All one will have to do is simply bend down and pick it up. As such, its presence does not depend on the worthiness of the recipient. Anyone who wants to is capable of receiving the wisdom.

This may partially explain why *Hashem* made it possible for me to impart this message. My part in its dissemination gives you the right to ask, "Who are you to say such a thing?"

Of course, my answer is: "You are right to question

me. My name does not mean anything. Please do not accept what I have written merely because it comes from me. Read it for yourself. If it strikes you as true and you incorporate it into your own outlook, then you will get full credit for the wisdom yourself. To prove that you wanted it for wisdom's sake, *Hashem* had to give it to you through a person with limited credentials."

Thus, the deteriorated situation of the times in which we live forces each of us to buckle down and reassess the situation *on our own*. That is what this generation is all about. And that explains the crux of the message and the purpose of this book; namely, you, dear reader, must discover yourself and become a self-made person. You must appreciate your role as a Jew and regain appreciation of Torah on your own.

Hashem is providing the wisdom in this book as a vehicle. It is up to you to pick it up and make use of it.

DEAR READER, I CAN ALREADY FEEL and sense the impressions you will have as you read this book. I know and feel the questions and emotional stirrings that will be dredged up within you. I went through — and, in fact, am still going through — the same set of feelings and questions. In fact, each time I reread and re-edit the manuscript, I am kept up at night.

As you read, you are sure to be stirred up. Forgive me

for doing that to you. You may be tempted to put down the book and not read further. However, I strongly recommend that you overcome such desires. I hope you will be courageous and read the book from cover to cover. By persevering, you will be able to make full use of all the suffering, both past and present. And suffering, as this book will endeavor to show, is meant to be fully used.

It may take you two or more readings to grasp the entire picture. You may find it helpful to first read two of our books — *Choose Life!* and *Days Are Coming* — whose content is related to this book. If you have questions, I will be more than happy to answer them once you have properly researched the entire book. You will find, in the end, that it was very rewarding to persevere through this study, as painful as it may be. Hopefully, above all, you will find yourself able to thank *Hashem* for every ounce of suffering, for every sigh, for every teardrop.

IN THE PAST, I HAVE BEEN ASKED to include some personal biographical information in one of my books. I have always been reluctant to do so. What will it really add? Why does one need to hear more stories and reminders of the Holocaust?

In the last four books, I did not feel ready or obligated

to share my past. However, in this book, where I am touching on so much hurt and inner feelings, perhaps I am obligated to share some of my personal experiences. What right do I have to hold back? Yes, some of these stories may only dredge up more pain. However, like a surgeon using a knife to cut into a patient, perhaps that pain is necessary for the ultimate good. If experienced within the context of this book, perhaps the pain will help the reader deal with his or her own pain all the more successfully.

The truth is that there really is something to be gained by reading stories of the Holocaust. When one looks into each story, a glimmer of light hiding in the darkness can be found. Whether they be stories of Jewish spiritual resistance and absolute adherence to Torah values, or stories which relate nothing more than the pain of those who suffered, there is something to be gleaned from each incident (see Chapters 5 and 6).

People ask, "How can you believe in *Hashem* after the Holocaust?"

In response, I say, "How can you *not* believe in *Hashem* after the Holocaust?"

I doubt that any survivor would deny that he survived only because of a continuous string of miracles that accompanied him day in and day out.[3] Understandably, people who did not go through the Holocaust have had a hard time envisioning how anything related to the Holocaust could be miraculous. Therefore, while I cannot possibly hope to relate even a fraction of the continuous miracles *Hashem* sent to my family and me, I realize the value in relating a smattering of personal incidents, if for no other reason than to make more palpable the experience of a survivor who had his faith in *Hashem* strengthened through suffering. With that in mind, I offer the following.

My Early Years Under Nazi Rule

I was born in Pressburg, Czechoslovakia in 1938, just before the outbreak of World War II. Even before the war, without firing a shot, the Nazis gained control over about one third of Czechoslovakia. Not long thereafter they took control over the entire country. Nevertheless, they did not begin deportation of the Jewish population to the death camps until 1942; and then the deportations were postponed until 1944 due to the efforts of my rebbi and teacher of later years, Rabbi Michoel Dov Weissmandel *zt'l*, who accomplished the deferment with a $50,000 bribe (as described in his book *Min HaMeitzar*).

During this postponement many Jews fled Czechoslovakia, including my entire family in 1943. We fled to neighboring Hungary, to the capital city of Budapest. Unfortunately, the Nazis soon took control of Hungary as well. In a short time, they began promulgating decrees against the Jewish population, including the mandatory wearing of a yellow star on all clothing. My parents knew from their experience in Czechoslovakia that after such decrees came the centralization of Jews into cramped ghettos, which in turn was soon followed by deportations. For this reason, they decided not to wear the yellow star, and instead managed to acquire papers which identified them as gentiles. The war was beginning to turn in favor of the Allies and they hoped they would not have to hold out too long.

During the entire time we pretended to be gentiles, we observed all the Torah laws down to their minutest details. As the eldest of my brothers, I was the only child who was told he was Jewish. The others were purposely kept ignorant because of the danger that would have resulted had they let something innocently slip from their lips. And I remember well, being tossed about on a sea of emotions — forced to live as a gentile in Nazi-occupied Europe, yet knowing full-well that I was a Jew. Experiencing these two worlds made an incredibly deep impression upon me.

Eventually our true identities were discovered. My grandparents, my aunts, and my mother were sent to Auschwitz, while my father and uncle were sent to a labor camp. We children — my three younger brothers and I — were distributed among various families and shelters in Budapest.

On her way to Auschwitz, my mother was in the advanced stages of pregnancy about to have her fifth child. In retrospect, her chances for survival were virtually nil. My grandparents and aunts who were deported with her did indeed perish. However, my mother made it to Auschwitz, gave birth there, and, although the baby did not survive, my mother did and was reunited with our entire family after the war. The baby girl my mother gave birth to in Auschwitz was the only member of our immediate family who did not survive.

Dear reader, as I begin to tell even the few stories I plan to relate here, I realize how ill-equipped I am, or, for that matter, anyone is, to convey even a fraction of the miracles performed during the Holocaust. How can I help but do great injustice to the actual experiences? My words, perforce, must fall woefully fall short of the actual deeds.

In those days, living under the shadow of Nazism, when people's lives literally hung in the balance from day to day, who could think of giving birth to children and raising them? However, my parents' attitude was, "We are Jews. We do what we have to do, and let *Hashem* do what He has to do." Who would believe that my three brothers and myself, my mother who gave birth in Auschwitz, and my father would all survive, and be reunited. Today, all, including the five children my parents had after the war, are living full Jewish lives, raising children who themselves are raising children.

That in itself is perhaps the greatest lesson: When we Jews go on living with complete faith, just doing what we have to do, all works out for the best. We do not have to make complicated calculations. A Creator runs the world.

As I explained earlier, despite our best efforts, we were discovered and separated from each other. My father, who had been placed in a labor camp, managed to escape — a miracle in its own right. He escaped, and risked entering Nazi-infested Budapest to locate his children.

One by one, despite the incredible odds, my father found all four of us, and for the next few months we hid successfully in various places. However, in the final weeks of the war, when the Russians were bombarding the city and our stomachs were bloated with hunger, we were forced to leave the relative safety of our private hideout and enter a public basement shelter.

As a rule, shelters like these were populated only by old gentile men and women. The young people had all been sent to the battlefront. My father, of course, could not afford to have himself sent to the front as a gentile because four little children were totally dependent upon him.

The cellar had three hundred beds stretched out one after the other. We lived there for days and days, and my father managed not to miss even one day of putting on *t'fillin*! He would put them on underneath the covers of his bed so that no one else would see, and would often bring me under the blankets to pray with him.

One day, while my father was underneath the covers,

wrapped in his *t'fillin* and praying, someone informed the authorities that a man was hiding in the cellar. As he lay beneath the blanket, two gestapo agents quickly entered the shelter and approached our bed. My father's sister, who had joined us, immediately understood the danger and placed us, the little children, on top of the bed. I was placed directly on top of my father's feet.

The Nazi looked into my eyes and said, "My little son, you are very suspicious looking to me." I just sat there stiffly, terrified, knowing full well what would await us should my father be discovered.

Again, the hand of *Hashem* saved us and the gestapo agents left without inspecting the lump beneath the covers.

Another incident occurred, though, where my father was not as lucky. A bomb exploded outside the shelter. People were hurt and killed. Others, including my father, ran to help. As he rushed up the staircase, another bomb exploded sending my father flying down the entire flight of stairs. He was badly hurt and momentarily lost consciousness. When he regained it, he thought the end was near. He called me to him, pulled me close, covered me underneath his blanket, and gave me his final will. I was six years old at the time.

"I don't think I can survive much longer," he said. "Your mother is in Auschwitz. I do not know if she is going to survive. You are the oldest of our children. The others do not even know that they are Jewish. You should know your brothers' real names are: Yitzchak Tzvi, Abba Chiya, and Yechiel. You must make sure they grow up to be Torah-observant. Remember, we Jews are going to outlive everyone. It is your duty to survive and remember what I am telling you forever."

Thank G-d, my father and my mother are still alive to this day, may *Hashem* let them live and be well till 120 years.

Miracle after miracle. And the miracles continued daily, until the war ended. Could someone who went through what we went through not have seen the hand of the Divine?

Emigration to the Holy Land

Almost immediately after we survived these tests, *Hashem*, in His kindness (yes, it was kindness, as this book will bear out), prepared a new set of difficulties and challenges.

In 1949, we came to the land of Israel, where my parents intended to settle permanently. I was eleven years old when we arrived. One of the first things I noticed was the disconcerting contrast to my previous experience. Under the worst conditions imaginable, my parents had sacrificed everything to maintain their practice of Judaism. In contrast, thousands and thousands of Jews were coming from around the globe — especially from Yemen and Morocco — to the Holy Land, where they cast off their Torah adherence without any resistance. For the first time in my life I saw Jews not satisfied with merely discarding Torah practice, but actively attacking Torah principles and Torah Jews.

I must say that the inner turmoil I went through during those years, from the age of 11 until 16, was enormous. So many young Jews were totally abandoning their heritage. I was in yeshiva, when one unforgettable incident happened.

An orphaned boy, a survivor of the death camps, lived in an orphanage and learned with me in one class. One day, his father — who was thought to have certainly perished in Europe — appeared. Living in Paris since the war ended, his father was an avowed Communist and atheist. I remember saying good-bye to my friend, realizing that he would soon be indoctrinated into his father's world — the Communist world. I remember that feeling of loss within me. I felt I was again experiencing a Holocaust — a spiritual one.

As you can imagine, those teenage years produced great conflict within me.

In America

My parents gave birth to five more children after the war. In 1950, they gave birth to a daughter. One year later, she contracted polio. At that time, the only place where she could receive treatment was in America. My father took her there, and stayed with her for two full years. During that time, my mother had to raise all the children alone. Finally, there was no choice. My little sister needed further treatment, and we all had to join her and my father in America.

After the Holocaust in Europe, the turmoil in Israel, we were cast into the spiritual wasteland of America.

My parents sent me to a yeshiva where I was able to remain insulated from the influences surrounding us. Furthermore, during two years in the Yeshiva of Nitra, in Mount Kisco, New York, I was privileged to learn in the presence of two outstanding rabbis. The first was Rabbi Yaakov Hornstein *zt'l*, recognized worldwide for his ability to penetrate the most complex topics of the *Gemara* and explain them with utmost clarity. In later years, I was able to apply his clear, analytical approach to everything from Torah *hashkafa* to current events.

My other mentor was the founder of the yeshiva, one of the great luminaries of this century, Rabbi Michoel Dov Weissmandel *zt'l*. Rabbi Weissmandel's Holocaust experience itself was particularly bitter. Packed into a cattle car heading for certain death, he managed to cut through the iron bars of a small window using a wire string and jump out of the speeding train. The cattle car continued to the death camp with his wife and family. They were gassed immediately upon their arrival.

Rabbi Weissmandel jumped from the train not to save his own life; but for the express purpose of informing the world of the Nazi atrocities in the hope of getting the railways bombed or some other relief enabling Jewish lives to be spared. He made contacts through letters and other means, yet, despite his best efforts, the world remained silent.[4]

He resettled in America, a broken man in many ways, yet filled with his unique brand of fire and determination to build anew. In my two years at his yeshiva, I was totally taken by his presence. I found myself in his every word. He spoke frequently in public and hardly a lecture went by that he did not break down into tears and sobs. One could feel his great pain.

Perhaps even greater than his pain over the past, was his pain over the present and the future of his people. He focused on how easy it was for a Jew to lose himself spiritually in American culture. He used to say, "Many of those early immigrants who came to America before World War I were greater than us." Then he would relate how he was told that in the Bais Medrash Ha-Gadol in the Lower East Side on Thursday night one could not find a seat. Everyone was packed closely together, learning Torah. Yet, most of the children of these people abandoned Torah observance. He would conclude, "And if we do not even come close to achieving their level of commitment, what will guarantee the future of our children?"

Those two years of study at his feet were extremely important to me. He taught that one must never trade off the truth for anything. When you see things clearly, go ahead with what you know to be correct despite the odds. (And no one confronted greater odds. In the face of a world dominated by brutal Nazis, he singlehandedly tried to save the lives of millions of Jews. Indeed, with $50,000 he bribed German officials in Czechoslovakia in order to postpone Jewish deportations for two years. Later, in the United States, he was not deterred by the incredible obstacles to setting up a yeshiva with European standards in the heart of rural America. His whole life was a lesson in dogged pursuit of Torah ideals regardless of the odds. Once he saw the truth, nothing stopped him.) From him I learned that without *Hashem*, nothing can be accomplished; and that with *Hashem* even the impossible could be achieved.

After two years in the yeshiva in Mount Kisco, *Hashem,* in His great kindness, helped me find my partner for life. I was not even 19 years old when I married and had to leave yeshiva in order to earn a living. Without skills or experience, I took a job as a truck driver down by the piers of Manhattan. The contrast in environments almost destroyed me at first. Only one month before, I was engulfed in Torah and holiness, protected under the wings of great rabbis; and now, I was surrounded by the filth and garbage of the piers of New York City.

"*Hashem*," I asked over and over again, "what do you want from me?"

I felt thrown to the wolves, drowning in a world so foreign and antithetical to everything I had been taught that I did not know how I could possibly survive. However, it was at that point in my life that I buckled down and dug deep into myself. I tried to recall all the teachings my rabbis had sought to instill in me. Until that point, it had all been abstract to me. Now I had to cash in on those teachings and learn to apply them, fast.

I immersed myself in the deep *hashkafa* books of our sages. *Hashem* saw my plight and helped me understand them. These books became my lifeline.

My personal favorites became the writings of the Ramchal (Rabbi Moshe Chaim Luzzatto, 1707-1746) and the Maharal (Rabbi Yehudah Loewe, c. 1512-1609). The Maharal, in particular, is the master of the homiletic (parable-like) teachings of the sages of the *Gemara* and *Midrash.* Throughout his works, I saw how the Maharal conveyed, in a positive way, the greatness of a Jew, the greatness of a test, the greatness of a difficulty. Over many years, I was able to see the influence of the Maharal on other great thinkers including the Baal HaṬanya, the Sfas Emes, and Rav Tzadok. In turn, these writings helped me understand the Maharal with greater clarity.

After years of effort, I attained enough mastery to teach in public for beginners and advanced Torah scholars. Whether it was the Maharal's book *Gevuros Hashem* — which explains the birth of the Jewish people in Egypt — or his *Tiferes Yisroel* — which teaches the essence of Torah and the revelation at Mount Sinai — or his *Netzach Yisroel* — which analyzes the benefit of exile and the ultimate redemption (upon which this book is based) — I saw the impact his teachings had on people.

The more I taught, the more I came to see the unifying thread in his approach. When I could finally say that I grasped, to some degree at least, the entire picture as the Maharal conveyed it, I could not help but just sit back in awe of the Creator's planning.

When you watch an artist begin a painting, it is hard to envision the outcome. The artist makes a line here, adds a color there, and none of it makes sense at first. However, after a while, you begin to see that a clear and beautiful picture is emerging. "Aha," you finally say. "I cannot get over how it all came together."

That is the feeling of understanding the Maharal, whose task it was to explain the words of our sages — the sages, whose goal was to lay down the meaning of the tapestry of creation. That is the effect I hope this book will have. I cannot guarantee that you will grasp the entire picture with one reading. However, I feel confident that a second or third reading — perhaps combined with a reading of *Choose Life!* and *Days Are Coming*, and with discussions with others or with me — will bring the overall picture into view for you.

Therefore, dear reader, do not throw your hands up in defeat if this book perplexes you. Just keep reading. Whatever you do not understand at the moment, pass by. Perhaps a later chapter will explain it to you. Perhaps a second reading or third reading will crystallize it for you.

I have already witnessed how effective the material in this book can be. When I lecture to groups of widows, childless couples, bereaved parents, divorcees, and others going through a personal holocaust, those who felt helpless, sad, and depressed left the lecture with their faces radiating joy. I am convinced that if you take the material in this book seriously, you can elevate yourself from whatever turmoil you are in.

"Give to the wise man, and he will become wiser."[5] My hope is that this book will be your first step toward comprehending the beauty within yourself, within your life, and within life's trials and tribulations. Then you can take that understanding and learn to become an artist who can paint his or her own picture and share it with others.

In Conclusion

I feel it is necessary to conclude with a story that summarizes and drives home the message of this book. This story was published in a book that I happened to be reading recently. Long before it was published, though, my family knew of the story because it involved my grandfather.

Reb Eliezer Landau was an assistant to the Belzer Rebbi, Rabbi Aaron Rokeach *zt'l.* Under the Nazi occupation, Reb Eliezer lived in the Buchner ghetto in

Poland. After the situation there had turned from bad to worse and then from worse to unbearable, he still had a chance to escape with his family. He asked the Belzer Rebbi for advice.

"Escape," the great rabbi told him. "Go to Hungary and you will survive."

"Rebbi," Reb Eliezer replied, "I am a Polish citizen. I do not know one word of Hungarian. We know that other Polish Jews that fled safely to Hungary were nevertheless caught, immediately returned to Poland, and killed. How can I think of doing the same?"

"Just go," the Belzer Rebbi said. "I give you a blessing that *Hashem* should help you."

Eliezer Landau went, he and his family. As they crossed by train into Hungary from the Austrian border, they had to disembark at the little town of Jur. The train station was buzzing with soldiers and police, and Reb Eliezer was afraid to open his mouth because by doing so he might reveal his identity to others. He wanted to buy tickets for a train to Budapest, but had no idea how he would be able to get them.

As he stood in the station house, feeling completely at a loss as to what to do, he spied a man with a beard. In addition to the beard, the man wore a white cap under which long hair flowed down to his shoulders. He looked like a typical Bohemian artist. All of a sudden, the "Bohemian artist" came over to Eliezer Landau and began speaking to him in Yiddish. They only exchanged a few words for fear that others might overhear. The man then bought train tickets to Budapest for himself, Reb Eliezer, and his family.

In the privacy of the train compartment, he finally began to speak. "Does your name happen to be Lazer Landau?" the man in Bohemian dress asked.

Eliezer Landau became pale. "How could you possibly know my name?" he asked.

"My name is Amrom Gestetner." (Amrom Gestetner was my mother's father.) "I live in Budapest. I am not what I appear to be. I dress as I do because I did not want to shave off my beard when I went into hiding as a gentile. Instead, I grew my hair long so I could look like a typical artist.

"My parents, may they rest in peace, were originally from Jur," he continued. "In fact, their graves are there. Today is my father's *yahrzheit.* However, I had no intention of going there, with so much danger about. However, last night I had a dream. I dreamed of the Belzer Rebbi, and he told me, 'Tomorrow is your father's *yahrzheit.* Go to his gravesite in Jur. In the train station there, you will find a Jew, with his family, whose name is Lazer Landau. He did many favors for me here in the ghetto. Please help him.'

"When I woke up this morning," my grandfather related to Eliezer Landau, whose eyes were bulging with amazement, "I did not know whether to take the dream seriously. However, today was indeed my father's *yahr-*

zheit and I decided to take this unusual dream to heart despite the danger. I had just returned from the cemetery when I saw you standing in the train station. It was then that I realized that the dream was true."

My grandfather took Eliezer Landau and his entire family to Budapest and hid them in his home for several months. He and his family survived the war and eventually settled in Israel.

This story is absolutely true. It is part of our family's firsthand experience. Who can say that *Hashem* did not perform miracles in the Holocaust? I am sure that every survivor has not only one, but many, many miracles to relate as to how he or she survived.

My family became even stronger believers after the Holocaust. We saw *Hashem* day in and day out. Hopefully by sharing these personal experiences with you, and then by transmitting to you the contents of this book, you, dear reader, will be able to strengthen your faith even in the midst of a personal holocaust you may be experiencing. May *Hashem* help each of us toward that end until the time comes for the *biyas go'ayl tzedek*, the coming of the righteous redeemer.

E.T.

OVERVIEW

This book is divided into seven chapters. The first three chapters introduce the reader to the benefit of suffering.

Chapter 4 discusses the main theme in greater detail, emphasizing the approach of the Maharal, and drawing significantly from his work *Netzach Yisroel* (Eternal Israel). For some readers, this chapter may be the most difficult to follow. Do not worry if you are one of them. Just keep reading and glean the *main* ideas, for they form the basis for understanding Chapter 5, which recounts several stories from the Holocaust. Chapter 5 is a key chapter in that it shows how the general principles laid down in the earlier chapters, particularly Chapter 4, apply to the specific circumstances of the Holocaust.

Chapter 6 draws parallels between the *akeida,* the "binding" of Yitzchak (Isaac), and the Holocaust. It discusses (among other topics) why a non-Torah Jew who was killed by the Nazis is nevertheless considered a *kodosh,* a holy Jew.

Chapter 7 focuses in on the personality of Rebbi Akiva, why he is the model for us — the Jew who suffers during the era of waiting for the *Moshiach* — and how we can gain consolation and understanding by examining the lessons his life provides.

The Appendix, in question and answer format, expands on the theme of suffering. Please note that the primary text contains references to relevant questions found in the Appendix. A glossary of Hebrew terms, bibliographical references, and information about Shalheves seminars, tapes, and books have also been provided.

DARKNESS BEFORE DAWN

CHAPTER 1

PRELUDE

EVERY GENERATION IS PLAGUED by its own nearsightedness. For centuries, though, and in fact for over three millennia, the Jewish people have been well-stocked with prophets and sages able to rise above the myopia of their times. They saw universal undercurrents in the otherwise obscure events of their day.

The post-Holocaust generation, however, has rightfully been called an orphaned generation. The Holocaust took not only six million Jewish lives, but countless Torah visionaries — the eyes of the generation. It has left us blind, bursting with questions and groping for answers.

Even in our orphaned status, though, there is hope. The Torah leaders of years past left records. These records were not merely clippings of the events in their times, but universal principles applicable to all times and in all places. Furthermore, in many instances, their remarks are directed to the future; advice intended specifically for an orphaned generation like ours, who would need to make sense of the insanity of their times without necessarily having access to a true visionary.

Our prophets and sages not only foresaw and foretold our suffering, but understood it better than we. Therefore, it is to our advantage to delve deeply into their words and understand the underlying principles in order to piece together a framework around which to understand the present.

One particularly relevant statement which *Chazal* make is recorded in the *Gemara*:[6]

> The world was created to last 6,000 years: 2,000 years of desolation and void (*tohu va'vohu*); 2,000 years of Torah; and 2,000 years [known as] *yimos HaMoshiach*, the era [literally, the "days"] of the Messiah.

In this statement, *Chazal* have provided us with a conceptual framework for understanding all world history.[7] The third 2,000-year period, *yimos HaMoshiach*, refers directly to our time — a time which we will now attempt to understand.

At this writing, it is currently the year 5752. Thus, 1,752 years of this 2,000 year era have elapsed without *Moshiach* arriving. How, then, can it be called "the era of *Moshiach*"?

The simplest answer is, as the *Gemara* explains, that the 2,000-year era of *yimos HaMoshiach* is a period particularly ripe for the arrival of *Moshiach* and the new world he will help usher in. His actual arrival, though, depends on criteria we have not yet met.

Paradoxically, the first 1,752 years of *yimos HaMoshiach* have been witness to unparalleled suffering, and the most severe persecution of the Jewish people. In reality, though, that is precisely the point. The emergence of the Messianic era, where peace is the catalyst for ever-widening knowledge of *Hashem*, is likened to the birth process. The time prior to the birth of this era is called *chevlai Moshiach*, literally, the "birthpangs of *Moshiach*." Just as there is an intimate connection between labor pains and birth, so, too, there is an intimate connection between suffering and redemption, between nearly 2,000 years of exile and the arrival of *Moshiach*. Exploring that connection is vital for understanding the times in which we live.

The Four Sons

Every *Pesach,* we read in the *Hagadah* about the four sons: the wise son (*chacham*), the evil son (*rasha*), the simple son (*tam*), and the son who does not know how to ask (*aino yodea lishol*). These four sons can be categorized into two pairs: the wise son with the simple son (*chacham* and *tam*); and the evil son with the one who does not know how to ask (*rasha* and *aino yodea lishol*). As the *Hagadah* details, the former pair ask questions related to the "how" of being Jewish. The latter ask questions related to the "why" of being Jewish.

Our generation is like the latter two: most Jewish people are either antagonistic toward their heritage or ignorant of it. The antagonistic ones ask questions to rationalize or perpetuate their antagonism, while the ignorant do not even care to ask. As the *Hagadah* tells us, it is the responsibility of the father to initiate the conversation with these two sons (the evil son and the one who does not know how to ask).

The last 80 years have inflicted upon us almost unparalleled suffering — World War I, World War II, the 1948 War, the Sinai War, the Six-Day War, the Yom Kippur War, and, most recently, the Gulf War, in addition to the interfighting and spiritual alienation we have suffered. Everything which has happened is actually a clear answer to an unasked question. Our job is to open up the conversation. When we ask the question properly, we can begin to appreciate the answer.

CHAPTER 2

THE QUESTION

To the uninitiated, suffering is synonymous with sin. It is a punishment for a prior committed wrong, one might think. Thus, many assume people suffer because they are bad and rejected by *Hashem*.

However, this is not so.

While it is true that *Hashem* created a world where one is rewarded for good and punished for bad, it would be superficial to understand suffering in this world as the exclusive result of some wrong-doing. Oftentimes, the "punishment does not fit the crime" — it is much worse. And, at other times, evil seems to go unpunished. It is obvious, therefore, that there is something more to suffering than mere reward and punishment.

The truth is that suffering is a prerequisite to the

acquisition of everything of value.

To bring a child into this world entails nine months of pregnancy and then labor pains (and then you have to raise the child). If you want to earn money, you must deprive yourself and work hard: "With the sweat of your brow you will eat bread."[8] You have to work for it, you have to sweat. David HaMelech said, "Sow with tears; harvest in song."[9] In other words, the amount of tears invested during the time of planting determines the degree of rejoicing and song during the time of harvest.

Everything of value in this world is first acquired through some type of suffering.[10] This is particularly evident regarding the Jewish people. No one people or nation has a comparable history of suffering. Yet, their suffering is directly connected to their promises of greatness.

The first time this connection is mentioned in the Torah is at the *bris bein habesarim*, the "Covenant Between the Parts,"[11] at which Avraham was told by *Hashem* that he would have descendants who would become *Hashem*'s special nation, the nation of Israel. *Hashem* then told Avraham:

> ". . . Know that your children are going to be strangers in a land not theirs, where they will be enslaved and oppressed for 400 years." (*Beraishis* 15:13)

The significance of this statement is magnified greatly when we consider that the Egyptian exile (the "strange land" where Avraham's children were to be enslaved for

400 years) was not just a one-time affliction. It was a precursor to, and incorporated within it, all four future exiles — the Babylonian (*Bavel*), Persian (*Madai-Pras*), Greek (*Yavan*), and Roman (*Edom*) exiles.[12] In fact, the ensuing command by *Hashem* to Avraham to sacrifice four types of animals in order to seal the "Covenant Between the Parts" is interpreted in the *Midrash* as an allusion to the four exiles.[13]

The implication is that the promise of having a special relationship with *Hashem* is connected to the decree of exile and oppression in a "strange land." Suffering, therefore, is more than just incidental to the Jewish people. It is at the heart of their formation, it is part and parcel of their being, and it is somehow connected to everything good they have been promised.

Thus, to view the suffering of the Jewish people as proof of the rejection of the once chosen people, or, similarly, to view it as evidence that *Hashem* does not control the world, is erroneous. On the contrary, if anything, the suffering of the Jewish people suggests the exact opposite: that they are indeed chosen and that *Hashem* is still very much in control of the world. Why else would the phenomenon of anti-semitism behave as an unalterable divine decree, being so irrational, impossible to eliminate, and so ever-present in every culture and time period in which the Jewish people have found themselves? What else would explain how the Jews have always outlived their oppressors? The incredible saga of the Jewish people supports the contention that they possess a unique standing in the world.

Jewish suffering is a by-product of chosenness, so much so in fact that, as strange as it may sound, the forefathers of the Jewish people chose suffering for their descendants! Before discussing anything else, let us investigate the sources which convey how three of Israel's faithful shepherds — Avraham, Yaakov, and Moshe — did indeed choose suffering for their progeny.

Avraham's Request

Hashem promised the aged, childless Avraham in the "Covenant Between the Parts" that his descendants would become as numerous as the stars. The Torah testifies that Avraham believed in *Hashem*, and *Hashem* considered it a mark of righteousness (*tzedakah*).[14] Immediately afterward, however, Avraham seemed to question *Hashem*'s promise. He said:

> "How will I know that my children will inherit this land which You have promised?" (*Beraishis* 15:8)

In response to Avraham's question *Hashem* told him:

> ". . . know that your children are going to be strangers in a land not theirs, where they will be enslaved and oppressed for 400 years and afterward they will go out with a great fortune." (*Beraishis* 15:13-14)

From *Hashem*'s response, we see that the Jewish history of exile was decreed. Now, if Avraham's question was a mistake, a statement of lack of faith in *Hashem*'s promise, then we may conclude that the sentence of exile for Avraham's children was a punishment.

However, Avraham's question was not a mistake. (See Question 9 in the Appendix.) This conclusion is immediately supported by the conspicuous statement which precedes his question: "And he [Avraham] believed in *Hashem*. . ." *Hashem* acknowledged Avraham's belief in Him! We can glean from this that Avraham's statement, no matter how it appears superficially, did not reflect a shortcoming in his faith.

Why then did *Hashem* decree exile for Avraham's children?

That is a question we will answer in full later. For now, it can be stated that he foresaw some benefit from their suffering. We may even go so far as to say that he wanted suffering for his children since we see he did not plead with *Hashem* to withdraw His decree, as he did when he was informed that *Hashem* planned to destroy the city of Sodom. As further proof, the *Midrash* informs us that *Hashem* asked Avraham to make a choice for his children: exile or *gehinnom,* and after careful deliberation he chose exile.[15] Avraham knew that, in his children's case, the suffering of exile would not be eternal. He knew that it would not be punishment for incorrectable evil. To the contrary, it was suffering that would ultimately benefit his children much more than had they not experienced it. And, therefore, he chose it for them.

Yaakov's Request

A similar process occurred with our forefather Yaakov.

Yaakov dreamed of a ladder which stood on the ground and reached into heaven. Angels went up and down the ladder.[16] In its analysis of this episode, the *Midrash*[17] teaches some of the most fundamental lessons of Jewish history. First, it tells us that the angels ascending and descending the ladder were the representatives of the nations who were to oppress Israel in the future exiles.

Yaakov saw the representative of *Bavel* rising 70 steps and then falling; and then he saw the representative of *Madai-Pras* rising 52 steps and falling; and then the representative of *Yavan* rising 180 steps and falling; and, finally, he saw the representative of *Edom*-Rome continue upward beyond sight. (The steps symbolized the number of years each of the nations would keep the Jews in exile. The continually evolving[18] exile of Edom, the only one which did not have a countable number, has already lasted almost 2,000 years.)

Next, the *Midrash* relates a verbal exchange between *Hashem* and Yaakov.

> When Yaakov saw the dream [of the angels, which represented future exiles and suffering for his descendants] he

became very frightened. "Is it possible that this angel of *Edom*-Rome will never fall down?" he asked.

Hashem told him, "Do not fear, My servant Yaakov. Even if he will come and sit next to Me, from there I will throw him down." This is the thought behind the verse of the prophet Ovadiah (1:4): 'If you [*Edom*] will rise like an eagle and make your nest among the stars, from there *Hashem* will throw you down.'

Hashem then told Yaakov to climb the ladder like the others. He became afraid. "They rose and eventually fell, perhaps my end will be like theirs," he said.

Hashem told him, "Do not fear. If you come up, you will never fall."

However, Yaakov doubted the guarantee, the *Midrash* says, and did not go up. *Hashem* said, "If you would have believed Me and gone up, you would never have fallen down. However, since you doubted My promise and chose not to go up, your children will be oppressed beneath the four exiling nations."

When Yaakov heard that, he became very afraid: "Will my children suffer forever?" he asked.

"No. I am going to help you from afar" — i.e. even if you will be scattered to the most faraway land, from there will I gather you. (See Question 10 in the Appendix.)

We learn from this *Midrash* that once Yaakov heard that his children would have to go through only a limited period of suffering, he had no complaints or regrets. He was at peace with the decision not to accept the invitation to go up the ladder.

Moshe

Chazal tell us that had Moshe been allowed to enter the land of Israel, he would have built an everlasting *Bais HaMikdash* and the world would have attained its final perfection[19] (and there would never have been a need for Jewish exile). However, when *Hashem* commanded Moshe to *speak* to a stone in order to miraculously bring forth water, Moshe *hit* the stone instead, prompting from *Hashem* the following response:

> "Because you did not believe in Me to sanctify Me, you are not allowed to enter the land of Israel." (*Bamidbar* 20:12)

This is the one shortcoming Moshe is cited for in the entire Torah, and it seems like such a small one. Even more strange, perhaps, is the teaching that Moshe prayed 515 times, imploring *Hashem* to let him enter the land. *Hashem* told Moshe not to say one more prayer or He would have to fulfill the request.[20]

Moshe was on the verge of entering the land and building the everlasting *Bais HaMikdash*. However, he hit the stone, and later refrained from praying for his entrance into the land, because that would have led to the building of the eternal *Bais HaMikdash*, something he knew would be unbeneficial for the people as they were.

In conclusion, then, we see that Avraham, Yaakov, and

Moshe turned down the opportunity to give their children an easy final redemption. In its place, they deemed that suffering would be more beneficial for their descendants — suffering resulting primarily not from punishment, but from decisions of the founders of the Jewish people. They understood that Jewish suffering somehow enhances and solidifies their special relationship with *Hashem*. It makes Israel into the *om segula*, *Hashem*'s treasured people.

However, why should that be? Why should the apparent removal of *Hashem*'s special providence over His people (i.e. allowing them to suffer and go into exile) be the dynamic which ultimately produces the closeness of the relationship? Exactly what unique benefit does suffering bring about?

That is the question.

As for the answer, it is first necessary to digress a little.

CHAPTER 3

RELATIONSHIPS OF LOVE

The Torah employs anthropomorphisms. That means it speaks of *Hashem* in the language of man.[21] It employs concrete analogies from the physical world in order to help us attain some grasp of the Infinite One.

For instance, when it uses the term "hand of *Hashem*" it does not mean that *Hashem* has a flesh and blood hand like a human being, but refers instead to *Hashem*'s overt manipulation of an event. Similarly, when Scripture ascribes an emotion to *Hashem*, we cannot presume to ultimately understand it. Human beings are filled with frailties and even our most exalted emotions are tinged with imperfections or shortcomings which, by definition, have no relationship to the Creator. Nevertheless, the Torah says, for instance, that *Hashem* loves or hates (as in "I loved Yaakov, but I hated Esav. . ."[22]).

Even though we can never ascribe to *Hashem* any of the frailties of man, since the Torah uses such terminology we must endeavor to understand the lesson inherent in such usage. We must seek to extract the implied message about how *Hashem* interacts with us and His world.

Let us analyze, for instance, the above-mentioned anthropomorphism that *Hashem* loves Israel but hates Esav. *Hashem* loves all of His creation with an unbounded love. The proof is that even though He, by definition, needs nothing, He created the world. Creation, then, is the ultimate altruistic act, the ultimate act of giving, because He created the world and He continues to sustain it despite needing nothing in return.

Thus, *Hashem* loves all creation.

Nevertheless, the Torah tells us again and again that, among all creation, *Hashem* has a special love for the people who keep His Torah and commandments, who keep His covenant:

> "[From] when Israel was a youth I loved him. . ." (Hoshea 11:1)
> "The word of *Hashem* to Israel. . . I have loved you. . . I love Yaakov. . ." (Malachi 1:1-2)

Hashem loves the people of Israel so much that He "hates Esav." Why does He "hate" Esav? Because Esav hates Israel, he hates Yaakov. And *Hashem* "hates" anyone who hates the one He especially loves.

That is the lesson for us. Even though *Hashem* is above human emotions, we have to know, and say with confidence, that *Hashem* loves Israel; He distinguishes Israel in a way He does not distinguish others. And, in fact, those who deny this distinction earn *Hashem*'s ire.[23]

Two Love Relationships

Hashem loves Israel. This love is expressed in the Torah in two basic kinds of relationships. On one hand, *Hashem* is a father: Israel is described as "children to *Hashem*";[24] "Sons of the living G-d";[25] and "My first born."[26]

At the same time, Israel has a marital relationship with *Hashem*.[27] "You will say [to Me], 'My Husband' . . . and I will betroth you forever . . ."[28] In *Shir HaShirim*, Israel's relationship to *Hashem* is characterized as the passionate yearning between a bride and groom. In that metaphor, the giving of the Torah on Mount Sinai is likened to the wedding between *Hashem* and Israel (as we will explain in the next chapter).

In order to better understand these two love relationships — parent and child and husband and wife — we have to understand the two ways we relate to *Hashem*, faith (*emunah*) and knowledge (*daas*).

Faith

None of us "know" that our parents are our parents. If they told you one day that you were adopted, you would have no defense. You could not deny it. According to Jewish law, if two valid witnesses testify that one is adopted, there is no way to deny it.

We only "believe" our father is our father and that our mother is our mother. It is not an experiential knowledge. We were not conscious of it when we were born.

While the relationship of child to parent is one based on belief, it has an advantage: as long as it is not contested, the bond between parent and child is the strongest bond possible, because a child can never be disowned. A parent can never truly say, "I divorce you; you are not my child any longer."

Knowledge

The second relationship of love, the marital relationship, is founded purely on knowledge, not belief. Both partners know and desire each other and intentionally arrange the marriage between themselves.

This relationship is stronger than parent to child because it cannot be contested — no one can come and tell you that your spouse is not your spouse. Both of you dated each other and were adults beneath the *chupah* (marriage canopy). Yet, at the same time, the marriage relationship can end in divorce. A spouse can say, "I no longer wish to be your spouse."

The Dual Relationship

Hashem declared in His Torah that the Jewish people, the children of Israel, are His children. Because the Torah says so, we "believe" it. However, belief is not the only characteristic of Torah Judaism. For, if the giving of the Torah would have been founded only upon belief, then the entire religion would be "belief founded upon belief" — a castle in the air.

Hashem, therefore, gave His Torah through direct, indisputable knowledge. First, He had Moshe predict and then carry out the ten plagues against Egypt, one after another. Then, He miraculously brought the Jews out of Egypt to the Red Sea, where He split the waters for them and drowned their enemies who were in hot pursuit. Then came the climax: the revelation at Mount Sinai, which was a simultaneous experience by *millions* of people. Every individual Jew, all of our ancestors, saw *Hashem*. It was experiential knowledge.

In essence, through the ten plagues, the exodus, the splitting of the Red Sea, and the revelation at Mount Sinai, *Hashem* made sure that the people of Israel were aware of Whom they were choosing to have a special relationship with. Like a bride beneath the wedding canopy, Israel was there willingly, with full awareness of Whom she was bonding herself to. And thus Scripture testifies: "I (*Hashem*) remember the devotion of your (Israel's) youth, your love as a bride, when you followed Me into the desert, a barren wasteland."[29]

Once it was established that the people of Israel received the Torah based on knowledge, in the manner of a bride, then the Torah's contents — the contents which tell them that they are children to *Hashem* — can never be contested. In other words, since the giving of the Torah is based on knowledge, everything which requires belief — everything we read in the Torah — is founded upon solid ground.

Thus, a Jew has both advantages: knowledge and faith. He exists in a marital relationship with *Hashem* which can never be contested, and he exists in a child-to-parent relationship with *Hashem* — a relationship which can never be severed, no matter how bad he is.

Let us go one step further now and understand these two types of love relationships (child and spouse) in a slightly different form: a prophet (*novi*) and a sage (*chacham*).

The Prophet and the Sage

Faith and knowledge are the primary characteristics, respectively, of the prophet and the sage. Prophecy is a gift from *Hashem* above and beyond the capacity of even the most refined human being. *Hashem* shows the prophet an entire picture independent of his human limitations.

Sagely wisdom, on the other hand, is wisdom acquired within the limits of human capacity and endeavor. (Of course, the sage also ultimately receives his insight from

Hashem. However, it is directly proportional to the ability *Hashem* gave him and the effort he exerted to acquire the wisdom.)

The *Gemara* tells us: *chacham odif mi'novi*, "a sage is greater than a prophet."[30] That means that knowledge conceived on one's own is stronger than knowledge received through the channel of prophecy. Although, quantitatively, prophecy shows one more than one could understand with one's own mind, qualitatively, anything perceived through one's own wisdom is greater. The fact that it was acquired through your ability, makes you appreciate it more.[31]

However, each approach has advantages and disadvantages.

The prophet's advantage is that there is no limit to what he can see since it is the Infinite One who shows him the vision. Furthermore, he receives the entire vision at once. He does not have to develop it piecemeal, like the sage.

The disadvantage is that the minute the vision — the picture — is withdrawn by *Hashem*, the prophet no longer possesses it. Think of a visit to the museum and looking at a beautiful piece of art. While gazing at it you enjoy it. When you leave, however, you cannot take it with you. You did not paint the picture. And, when you go, the enjoyment is gone.

The real disadvantage of prophecy is that the recipient does not necessarily become one with the inner part of the prophecy's message. He did not make the vision himself. It was bestowed upon him. Therefore, it does not take root as deeply as self-initiated wisdom and, consequently, its effect is not necessarily long-lasting.

However, the sage, too, has a disadvantage. His insights do not come to him with the same magnitude and breadth with which a prophet receives his insight. Nevertheless, the sage has an advantage. Whatever he does perceive cannot be taken away from him. He worked on it. Therefore, although the sage does not get his wisdom in the same quantity and magnitude as the prophet, the wisdom he does get is more a part of him.

Of course, the ideal is to possess the benefits of both sagely wisdom and prophetic wisdom. In fact, our greatest prophets possessed sagely wisdom, and our greatest sages possessed a knack for supernatural insight.

As it is on an individual level, so, too, is it on a national level. *Hashem* desired that His people possess both types of wisdom. Therefore, He prepared two experiences: 2,000 years of Torah (through prophecy) and 2,000 years of the era of the *Moshiach*, *yimos HaMoshiach* (through sagely wisdom).

Clearing the Way for the Sage

The epitome of the 2,000 years of Torah was the Generation of the Desert. This generation experienced the miraculous exodus from Egypt (*yetzias Mitzraim*), the parting of the Red Sea (*kriyas yam suf*), the revelation at

Mount Sinai (*matan Torah*), the manna from heaven for 40 years in the desert, and other obvious miracles. They are therefore called a *dor daiah*, a "generation of knowledge." *Hashem*'s power was unmistakingly shown to them. They *knew* Him from first-hand experience. They did not have to *believe* exclusively in the words of Moses, or of any other individual.[32]

The epitome of these miraculous experiences was the revelation of *Hashem* at Mount Sinai. Millions of people, simultaneously, were given a picture which included everything: who *Hashem* was, who they — the Jewish people — were, what their mission would be, their destiny, etc. That picture was flashed to them by *Hashem*. Everyone knew *Hashem* and heard His words.

As explained by Rabbi Yehudah HaLevi, in his classic of Jewish philosophy called *The Kuzari*, at the Red Sea and Mount Sinai the Jewish people reached the same level of prophecy as Moshe. And as the *Midrash* tells us, even the simplest handmaidens saw visions like the prophet Yechezkal.[33] The people, taken as a whole, were privy to knowledge which came to them with the force of prophecy, and they therefore compare to the prophet.

Despite this, however, as we shall explain, they lacked the benefit of knowledge obtained through the medium of *chachmah,* natural wisdom. Consequently, *Hashem* prepared an era compared to the sage. That is the 2,000-year era of *yimos HaMoshiach*, the era we are currently in. The purpose of this era is to give the Jewish people the opportunity to acquire Torah through their own labor. To do so, everything which had been previously given to them during the 2,000 years of Torah had to be swept away.

And it was.

In addition to the dissolution of the Jewish government and societal infrastructure in the land of Yehudah (Judea), the *Bais HaMikdash* was destroyed, and with its destruction, prophecy ceased. Lacking *Bais HaMikdash* and land, the national character of Israel vanished. Everything characteristic of the glory days of Israel was stripped away. Thus was ushered in the 2,000-year era of *yimos HaMoshiach*.

The previous 2,000 years, the years of Torah,were like one great prophetic flash. However, the flash passed. The experience ended. It is the design of the ensuing 2,000 years, up to and including our times, to reacquire and develop the flash just as the sage does: through working with our own resources within our own limits.

Thus, the beginning of this 2,000-year period coincides with the redaction of the *Mishnah* by the group of sages known as the Tanaiim. The era of the Tanaiim was followed by the era of the Amoraiim. Together, the Tanaiim and the Amoraiim constitute the body of sages who edited and anthologized the *Gemara*, the entire body of oral teachings. That monumental effort at the beginning of the latter 2,000-year period represents the epitome of the groundwork of the sage.

Of course, the *Gemara* was not created by the Tanaiim and Amoraiim. Their main function was to transcribe the oral tradition as it had existed since Mount Sinai. Nevertheless, they were given leeway to recover elements of the tradition that had become vague through the use of their natural wisdom.

The sage gains on his own everything that was originally given to the prophet. And he does so in the vacuum of exile. In fact, it is the vacuum which creates the possibility for him to utilize his sagely wisdom.

This explains the purpose behind Jewish suffering during the last 1,752 years, *yimos HaMoshiach*. It is a sweeping away of everything previously held sacred for a specific goal: to pave the way for an Israel which has gained its status through its own efforts and sacrifices; an Israel which possesses the advantages not only of the prophet but of the sage as well.

The Representatives of Each Era

The archetypal leader — the *Rebbi* — of prophecy was Moshe. "There was no prophet like Moshe"[34] — he is our teacher. Therefore, the Torah was given through him. And the 2,000 years of Torah are characterized by him. Corresponding to Moshe, the archetypal leader, the *Rebbi*, of the era of *Moshiach* is Rebbi Akiva.

Rebbi Akiva lived during the generation when the light of Torah knowledge was beginning to become darkened by the oncoming night of exile. He was one of the *asara harugai malchus* — the ten sagely martyrs who were tortured to death at the hands of the Romans. Originating from the darkest beginnings himself — he was a descendant of the evil general Sisera[35] — Rebbi Akiva was an unlearned Jew, antagonistic toward the Torah and its sages, until the age of 40. Nothing was given to him — he started from scratch. Then he began to grow and learn and climb until he became not only the Torah luminary of his time but for all ensuing times. He eventually scaled so high, the *Midrash* tells us, that when Moshe saw prophetically how great he would be, Moshe asked *Hashem* to give Rebbi Akiva his mission![36]

In reality, Moshe saw that Rebbi Akiva was his counterpart: just as he, Moshe, was the prototype of prophetic wisdom, Rebbi Akiva was the prototype of sagely wisdom.

Influx of Knowledge in the Modern Age

Just as Rebbi Akiva, the last generations of the era of the *Moshiach* must begin with nothing. Thus, they must be the most suffering, orphaned generations because everything previous will have been swept away. They will have to discover *Hashem* and reaffirm their commitment to Him on their own. The final generation will acquire on its own the level of knowledge given to the Children of Israel on Mount Sinai.

We see this borne out in the explosion of knowledge

in our times. For instance, today we have the ability to demonstrate the divinity of the Torah through programming computers to locate the hidden "Codes."[37]

The existence of the Codes was first revealed in our times by Rabbi Michoel Dov Weissmandel *z'tl.* These codes are words, phrases, and sentences embedded as single letters spaced at consistent intervals throughout the Hebrew text (for example, every 50th letter). These codes are superimposed on each other and exist within the readable text without obscuring the well-known Biblical narrative. Yet, they spell out information directly related to the location in which they are found — information not only of Biblical events, but post-Biblical events including the modern day.[38]

Woven like an intricate tapestry throughout the 3,300-year-old text, the probability that any one of these patterns happened by chance is astronomical. As one computer specialist turned believer through exploration of the Codes explained, "One can more easily believe that ten chimps left alone for one hundred years with a word processor could accidentally write a Shakespearean play. The probabilities . . . are ridiculously outside the realm of mathematical reasonableness."

Similarly, breakthroughs in science (contrary to the belief of many) have lent greater credibility to the existence of a Creator. Even the leading evolutionist Professor George Wald is at a loss to explain how chance could be responsible for the incredible complexity of the scientific discoveries in his field of expertise. He writes, for instance:[39]

> Organic molecules therefore form a large and formidable array, endless in variety and of the most bewildering complexity. One cannot think of having organisms without them. This is precisely the trouble, for to understand how organisms originated we must first of all explain how such complicated molecules could come into being. And that is only the beginning. To make an organism requires not only a tremendous variety of these substances, in adequate amounts and proper proportions, but also just the right arrangement of them. Structure here is as important as composition — and what a complication of structure! The most complex machine man has devised — say an electronic brain — is child's play compared with the simplest of living organisms. The especially trying thing is that complexity here involves such small dimensions. It is on the molecular level; it consists of a detailed fitting of molecule to molecule such as no chemist can attempt.

The closer we come toward the end, the more the valve of natural wisdom is opened. The Zohar long ago predicted:[40]

> In the 600th year in the sixth millennium [i.e. the year 5600, i.e. 1840 C.E.] the gates of supernal knowledge above will open, along with the wellsprings of knowledge below.

In the secular world, this coincides approximately with the Industrial Revolution. And although mankind has the free will to use the influx of knowledge for good or bad — and the thrust of most nineteenth century thought was to deny *Hashem* — knowledge in all fields is flooding the world like never before.

This is not coincidence. It is the prerequisite to the Messianic era. Every piece of knowledge which previously had come into the world through the revelation at Sinai and prophecy is made available through natural channels. The challenge of our day and age is to rediscover it from the ground up, through wisdom, through our own research.

Therefore, we are witness in our time to the Teshuva Movement, an unprecedented return of young people to their Jewish roots from families and societies which were ignorant of or antagonistic toward Torah values. What has attracted them back to the fold? The Codes, science, logic — in a word, "knowledge." And their need for knowledge is fortifying foundations traditionally constructed primarily with the material of faith.

This idea is enunciated in Isaiah: "For [then] the whole earth will be filled with the knowledge of *Hashem*."[41] Everything which previously had been transmitted only through belief will be understood with knowledge, i.e. "filled" up with knowledge. A *hollow* is created when a giver gives but the receiver has not fully received. That is the *hollow* created by *Hashem* giving knowledge to us miraculously from above. We had not labored for it yet. That hollow, though, will be "filled" one day, as the prophet says, with knowledge obtained from below through the human struggle to obtain sagely wisdom.

That process produces the excitement we see in new returnees. As the Rambam writes: "The more you know *Hashem*, the more love of *Hashem* you have."[42] Today's generation actually relates better to love of *Hashem* than fear of *Hashem*. All they need is knowledge. When Torah observance emanates only from belief and prophecy, the relationship to *Hashem* relies primarily on fear. However, the closer we get to knowledge, as the Rambam notes, the more important a role love of *Hashem* plays.

The Answer

It is now time to restate the question and answer it in full: What is the benefit of suffering? Specifically, what is the benefit of Jewish suffering? What it has taken from us is abundantly clear; what has it done for us?

The 2,000-year era of Jewish suffering is designed to allow the Jewish people to procure on their own that which was given to them during the 2,000-year era of Torah. At Mount Sinai, the epitome of the 2,000 years of Torah, *Hashem* introduced Himself as follows:

> "*Anochi Hashem Elokecha* . . ." I am *Hashem* your G-d . . . (*Shmos* 20:2)

Anochi, the Hebrew word for "I," is an expression of self that reflects the essence greater than *ani*, which also means "I" but does not necessarily reflect the essential self. The greatest revelation of *Hashem* that the world has ever seen took place at Mount Sinai. And that revelation is introduced and characterized with *anochi*.

Later in the Torah, *Hashem* says:

> "*Anochi hastir astir es ponai.*" 'I (*anochi*) will surely hide My face.' (*Devarim* 31:18)

This verse, which refers to the 2,000 years of *yimos HaMoshiach*, reveals to us that although a time will come when Hashem will appear hidden, His *anochi* — His essential self — will still be present. It was as if *Hashem* was saying, "My *anochi* will become hidden in the dark exile of the 2,000 years of *yimos HaMoshiach*. Yet, even there, in the darkest of darknesses, it will still exist, as it always has and always will, so that those who seek it will be available to find it."

If the original gift from *Hashem* of the 2,000 years of Torah had not been withdrawn, there would have been no chance to reacquire Torah through our own struggles and efforts. Therefore, if the era of Torah implied miracles, prophecy, and closeness to *Hashem*, then the era of our attempt to recover Torah implies setbacks, darkness, and exile. And that explains why it appears that *Hashem* has hides from us. In reality, He watches from the sidelines and longs for us to succeed. However, for our own benefit, He refrains from interfering.

The climax of the 2,000 years of Torah occurred at the beginning, with Moshe and the generation of the desert; the climax of the 2,000 years of *yimos HaMoshiach* will occur at the end, with the arrival of *Moshiach*. The 2,000 years of Torah peaked at the beginning and then tapered off; the 2,000 years of *yimos HaMoshiach* will initially continue that tapering off process, and, only near the very end, peak. Whereas the 2,000 years of Torah produced a revelation of Hashem's greatness, the 2,000 years of *yimos HaMoshiach* will produce a revelation of the Jewish people's greatness — of their devotion to the revelation of the *anochi* of *Hashem* even in the midst of dark exile.

Suffering is the process of revelation of self, of the discovery of powers of self which otherwise lay dormant. Avraham, Yaakov, and Moshe understood this when they elected to have their children suffer in the darkness of exile. Avraham himself suffered enormously. He was imprisoned many years for his beliefs and then thrown into a fiery furnace (from which *Hashem* miraculously saved him). He was estranged from his father and exiled from his homeland. He had to banish his son and the boy's mother from his own house. He had to hide his wife from the authorities twice for fear of their lives. He was the only monotheist in a world of paganists, truly alone in the world. And finally, at the climax of his life, he had to obey *Hashem*'s command that he sacrifice the son he waited 100 years to have. Through all his suffering, though, Avraham never complained. In fact, his love of *Hashem* grew great during these trials because he knew that his suffering was making him into a self-made spiritual giant.[43]

Avraham wanted suffering for his children for the same reason. He wanted them to inherit that self-made stature, which could only come through suffering, the removal of supports which lesser people depended upon. Therefore, he had no regrets over *Hashem*'s response that his children would suffer as strangers in a land not their own for 400 years (and then the ensuing four exiles), because deep down he knew that exile would ultimately bring out the very best in them.[44]

The last 2,000-year era of exile represents a drop to the bottom of an unfathomable abyss. The deeper we go into the thick darkness, the more we grope for the rays of light which once lit our way. In our groping for answers we begin to appreciate what we had. As the darkness thickens we begin to crave the light even more. We start fighting to get it back, from the ground up, from wherever we are, despite our suffering.

When we recapture everything we originally lost, then we will be complete; our Torah will be a complete Torah. Faith and knowledge, prophet and sage, will all become one. We will have matured from a child into a beloved wife, a wife who shares a special intimacy with her beloved that not even a child shares with its parents. That intimacy is a maturing of knowledge, of experience, of wisdom which is hard to earn. Nevertheless, in the end, the congregation of Israel's maturation from the status of merely a child to *Hashem* into the status of a wife to *Hashem* will prove worth everything ounce of suffering. Thus, the benefit of this extended and mind-boggling period of suffering is the emergence of Israel's truest and deepest self.

Applying It to the Individual

The approach we have depicted contains the insights necessary for the individual to overcome his or her suffering. There are many obvious parallels between the suffering of the community and the suffering of the individual. When the individual understands that the tragedies which have befallen the Jewish people are for the good, he or she will be able to apply that knowledge to his or her personal situation. Identifying with the collective suffering is an important step on the path toward individual redemption.

Stop and Think

Of course, even with this knowledge, it is not easy. A natural reaction to the pain of suffering is to ask: Why? If you find no answers, it is likely that the very question "Why?" causes pain. And when it does, you tend to seek "tranquilizers" to kill the pain (just as it is natural to seek a drug when physical pain strikes).

Some turn to alcohol and become alcoholics. Others turn to work and become workaholics. Still others find other addictions and distractions. Whatever the tranquilizer of choice, a pain-killer is not a cure. When we are stricken with something unexpected, the first step toward true recovery is to realize that the affliction was meant to make us stop and think.

Stop and think.

Hashem is capable of anything. If we are talking about a Being Who created both the atom and the distant stars, Who animates the particles which circle the atom and gives motion to the distant stars, Who gave us intelligence and knows our deepest thoughts, then we are talking about a Being Who can do anything. Anything less is not *Hashem*.

Therefore, *Hashem* is certainly capable of taking away suffering — or preventing it in the first place. Why then does He allow us to suffer?

For our sake.

When *Hashem* told Avraham to sacrifice Yitzchak, it was a test which would have crushed all but the greatest human being. However, the Creator does not give someone a test he cannot handle. He knew Avraham was up to the test.

If *Hashem* knew that Avraham would pass the test, then why did He test him?

For Avraham's sake — to let Avraham, as well as the

whole world, know the righteousness in his soul. As the Ramban remarks: "The benefit of a test is for the one who is tested."[45]

Hashem only tests the righteous. Evil people do not get tested. Suffering brings out the deepest, most sublime greatness lying dormant in the human heart, and only the righteous are worthy of it. The evil do not usually suffer. And when they do, it is often only at the end of a career of power, prestige, and desires fulfilled. Their suffering is more than likely a final punishment.

"When the wicked [and their wickedness] sprout like grass, it is only so that they should be cut down forever."[46] The initial pleasure and success that the wicked oftentimes experience are, in reality, part of their punishment. They are receiving full payment for the few good deeds they may have performed. When their account is paid, though, the punishment inflicted upon them is final.

On the other hand, when the righteous suffer, they are gaining. Their spiritual "bank account" is growing daily and accruing interest. The payoff will occur at some future date in a way they can benefit from forever.

Hashem can help the one who suffers and He can relieve suffering at any moment. However, the suffering is also a form of His help. It will make the good person better than he or she was.

If one stops and thinks, and hasn't already overdosed on tranquilizers, he will recognize that suffering, too, comes from *Hashem*. With this recognition, the first and perhaps most difficult obstacle is overcome. The pang may still remain, but the fatalistic feeling should not. Turn to *Hashem* to lighten or remove the suffering, but the point is: *turn to Hashem*. Do not overdose on tranquilizers. Realize that suffering has a purpose.

CHAPTER 4

THE MARRIAGE BETWEEN HASHEM AND ISRAEL

Baruch atoh Hashem . . . haMikadaish es amoh Yisroel al y'dia chupah v'kiddushin, "Blessed are You *Hashem* . . . who sanctifies His people Israel with *chupah* and *kiddushin*."

(Marriage blessing)

We have the basic answer to our question: the suffering of the 2,000-year *yimos HaMoshiach* era is destruction for the sake of building. We are stripped of a self given us by *Hashem* for the express purpose of ultimately regaining that self through our own efforts and inner powers. *Hashem* is maturing the Jewish people, preparing us to be His eternal partner eternally bonded to

Him.

The benefit of suffering is one of the most important teachings of Judaism, and has been a basic part of Jewish literacy since Avraham. It is only in this century, perhaps, that this lesson has been lost for the majority of Jews. The Holocaust and events in the post-Holocaust world have played a great part in that deterioration of understanding. Therefore, it is particularly apt and essential to reteach this lesson so that the last 50 years (at least) of Jewish suffering are seen within a conceptual framework true to Torah designed to enhance its understanding.

One of the absolute masters of Jewish thought during the past 500 years is the Maharal of Prague. He not only explained cryptic rabbinic teachings and obscure *Midrashim*, but pieced together from them a distinctive system of thought. Where we, in our spiritual poverty, see bits and fragments, the Maharal makes connections and profound inferences. He shows us how the thought-world of the great Jewish sages is really one.

Given the foundation for understanding the benefit of suffering laid in the earlier chapters, let us now turn in detail to the framework of Jewish suffering as perceived by the Maharal. In the next chapter, we will show how the Holocaust fits into that framework. First, however, we must delve deeply into the idea of the Jewish people's relationship to *Hashem* in the sense of a marital relationship.

Hashem and Israel in Marriage

The marriage process entails three steps. The first step, the *vort,* is the couple's declaration of their desire to be married. Next comes the official engagement. Finally, the couple is married in a ceremony beneath the *chupah.* (The *chupah* is where the union between husband and wife first occurs. This union is not merely contractual or economic. Husband and wife are actually viewed as half-souls. Through marriage they literally become one, as they were originally.[47])

Each of the three stages of a wedding has a parallel in the history of the people of Israel and their marriage to *Hashem.* The *vort* was the "Covenant Between the Parts" (*bris bain habesarim*), the engagement was the exodus from Egypt (*yetzias Mitzraim*), and the wedding was the giving of the Torah on Mount Sinai (*matan Torah*).

The Vort

At the *vort,* the "Covenant Between the Parts,"[48] *Hashem* made a pact with Avraham to give his offspring the mission to complete the purpose of creation.[49] This was a declaration of intention to carry out a union between two parties, similar to a couple's declaration to get married.

Also, as noted previously, at the "Covenant Between the Parts" *Hashem* told Avraham that his children would be enslaved and oppressed for 400 years. This is puzzling, though, given the nature of this pact between

Hashem and Avraham.

When a member of a royal family intends to marry a poor girl, the first thing he does is arrange to have beauticians, cosmeticians, and other personnel help make the girl presentable. Only afterward is the engagement party arranged.

Hashem did just the opposite. He told Avraham, "Know" that before the marriage will take place (at Mount Sinai), I will exile your children to a place like an "iron furnace" for 400 years, where they will lose everything. All the beauty in you Avraham — and in Yitzchak, Yaakov, and his sons — will be lost. They will be stripped bare of all they will inherit from you. When they hit rock bottom, "the forty-ninth level of defilement," I will immediately lift them out and bring them to Mount Sinai where I will marry them. Mount Sinai will be their *chupah.*

In other words, through physical and spiritual oppression in ancient Egypt, *Hashem* made the *kallah* (bride) Israel as unpresentable as possible. This is the puzzling condition which *Hashem* made with Avraham at the "*vort*" called the *bris bain habesarim.*

The Maharal, though, explains the idea. When an argument ensues between a couple shortly after they marry, the husband is likely to claim, "When I dated you, you were at your best. You were always smiling. You always dressed beautifully. But now that I see you every day, as you really are, I'm shocked. It's not the you I knew before." In Jewish law, this is akin to a claim of *mekach ta'oos*, a sale under false impressions.

As the Maharal explains, *Hashem* sent Avraham's offspring into dark exile in Egypt to eliminate His ability to make a claim of *mekach ta'oos*. He said to Avraham, "I'll marry your children under such circumstances that no matter how low they sink, they will never be as ugly and as empty of virtue as they were in Egypt."

That was *Hashem*'s design in bringing the Jewish nation down to such a low level. And that was the underlying idea behind the *vort,* the first of the three stages of Jewish marriage.

The Engagement and the Chupah

At the second stage, *Hashem* officially engaged Himself to His people — He took them out of Egypt. Beforehand, they were slaves to Pharaoh. Afterward, they were designated solely for *Hashem*.

The third stage, the giving of Torah on Mount Sinai, is equivalent to the *chupah* (wedding) between *Hashem* and Israel. This *chupah* has two parts: *kiddushin* and *nisuin. Kiddushin* is the giving of the ring. *Nisuin* is the final ceremony. The *Midrash* tells us that when *Hashem* "married" Israel, He held Mount Sinai over them as a *chupah.*[50] (This will be discussed later in detail.) If holding the mountain held over their heads like a *chupah* was the *nisuin,* then what part of the experience at Mount Sinai represented the *kiddushin*?

Kiddushin is performed with a wedding ring. Placing it on the *kallah*'s finger, the *chasan* (groom) says, "With this you become sanctified (*m'kudeshes*) to me." The ring, in essence, is the instrument of unity.

At Mount Sinai, the instrument of unity — the ring — between *Hashem* and Israel was the tablets of the ten commandments (the *luchos*). Through them the Jewish people became united with *Hashem*.

The *luchos* actually represent the entire 613 commandments of the Torah. Through keeping the Torah we become one with our Maker, with our other half. ". . .You chose us from among all the nations and gave us the Torah."[51] Through giving us the Torah, *Hashem* married us.

The Mountain Over Their Heads

Now, regarding the *nisuin, Chazal* tell us that *Hashem* held the mountain over Israel and said, "If you do not accept the Torah, this is where you will be buried!"[52] Why did *Hashem* have to issue an ultimatum? What is gained by such force? Just prior to this event, the Jewish people answered *Hashem*, "[Whatever You say] We will do and listen."[53] They were ready to accept the Torah without any questions. Why did *Hashem* have to use force?

To appreciate the difficulty, imagine a wedding. The *chasan* and *kallah* are standing beneath the *chupah*. Everything is ready for them. They are both excited.

Suddenly, when it comes time for the *chasan* to take out the ring, he not only takes out a ring but a gun as well and tells his *kallah*, "Take the ring. Otherwise, I will kill you!"

She replies, "I do not understand. I am here because I want to be here. I want to marry you. What is the point of pulling a gun now underneath the *chupah*?"

That (*k'viochol*) is what *Hashem* did!

There are different answers to this dilemma. Let us briefly explain three of them.

The first answer is given by the *Midrash*:[54] The Jewish people said, "We will do and we will listen" only with regard to the written Torah. However, they were unwilling to accept the oral Torah, which future rabbis would interpret. That is why *Hashem* had to force them.

A second answer is given by the *Tosafos* commentators:[55] The people said, "We will do and we will listen" a few days before receiving the Torah. The Torah, though, was given later amidst lightning, thunder, and the quaking of the earth. This display of power was meant to impress upon the people that the existence of the world, the very purpose of creation, was dependent upon Israel's acceptance of the Torah. Therefore, since it would be natural for them to have second thoughts about taking on such a weighty responsibility, there was a real chance that the people, who had been so genuine in their desire to keep Torah just a few days before, would lose their nerve. Consequently, *Hashem* lifted the mountain as if to say, "There will be no turning back at this point." Although they had volunteered earlier, He held the mountain over them so that they would not get "cold feet."

The Maharal, based on a *Midrash,* interprets the passage in a third, very unique manner.[56] In Jewish law, if a man rapes a woman, one of the punishments is that he must marry the woman (if she wants) and forfeit of his right to divorce her. *Hashem* binds Himself to the laws He set forth in His Torah. He forcibly married the Jewish people, the Maharal explains, *in order to give up His right to divorce them.* He lifted the mountain over them. He forced them, and forevermore gave up His right to divorce them.

The Element of Force

According to the Maharal, the way *Hashem* conducted the "marriage" to His people indicated that His desire was irrevocable. A problem remains. Even though *Hashem* expressed His irrevocable desire to wed the Jewish people, did the Jewish people show an irrevocable desire to be married to Him?

This question is particularly important because the first principle of marriage requires that both parties desire to be married to each other *of their own free will.* There can be no element of force. However, when exploring the sources in detail, it becomes obvious that *Hashem* forced the marriage from His end — so much so that it would seem virtually impossible for the Jewish people to express their desire even if they wanted to. Consider the following:

1) As we said, *Hashem* held Mount Sinai over the Children of Israel and said, "If you accept the Torah, fine; if not, this is where you will be buried!" It was as if a *chasan* told his *kallah*, "If you marry me, fine. If not, you are dead." The woman in that case does not even need a *gett*. The marriage is not a marriage. Therefore, how is the *kallah*, Israel, bound to this wedding?
2) The Maharal interprets the holding of the mountain over Israel's head in a unique way. He understands it in a positive light, not as an ultimatum. Explaining the words of *Chazal* on a figurative level, the Maharal writes that the experience at Sinai was so powerful that there was no other choice but for Israel to accept *Hashem* as their "Husband." How could people who experienced the miraculous revelation at Mount Sinai not accept *Hashem* as their *Hashem*? It was *as if* the mountain was held over them.

Even with this understanding, the question remains: Whether Mount Sinai was held over Israel's head literally or figuratively, it was still held over their heads. In either case, the implication is that free will was somehow diminished. If that is so, the validity of the entire marriage is in question.

3) This third explanation differs from the previous one only in terms of emphasis. It was not so much the miraculous events which seduced Israel into accepting the Torah at Mount Sinai, but the beauty of the *Chasan* Himself. At the Red Sea, the people were compelled to say, "This is my G-d, and I will beautify Him."[57] Even fetuses in the wombs of their mothers said, "This is my G-d, and I will beautify Him."[58] At the Red Sea, *Hashem* opened all the seven heavens and revealed Himself.

This manifestation of the Creator's beauty was actually a kind of inducement used by *Hashem* to persuade Israel to accept the terms of the union. When *Hashem* revealed His unbelievable beauty, how could anyone decline? And if Israel could not decline, then how could this kind of wedding be binding? It was seduction.

Both force and seduction are unacceptable means to marriage. In either case, the implication is that the people of Israel accepted the Torah on Mount Sinai with outside interference. If so, where is the free will of the *kallah*? Where is there room for her to marry with full consent, of her own free will?

4) *Hashem* took Israel out of Egypt and supported them in the desert before leading them to Mount Sinai. Under natural circumstances, millions of people locked in the desert cannot survive. There-

fore, *Hashem* provided the "Clouds of Glory," the well of Miriam, and the manna from heaven. Every form of sustenance — shelter, water, food — came directly from *Hashem*.

After three weeks of this "menu," fully isolated from the world, totally dependent upon Him, *Hashem* "asked" Israel if they wanted to "marry" Him. Of course they said "Yes." How could they say otherwise? If He would have halted any of the miracles, the people would have perished. So, again, there was an element of compulsion.

5) When *Hashem* took Israel out of Egypt and isolated them, He separated them from the nations; they became a "married woman," bound to one Husband. They became the chosen people.

Isolation reduces free choice. The ability to commingle, discuss, and make comparisons with others is necessary for informed, independent decision-making. If *Hashem* isolated Israel in the desert, how did they have the free will necessary to make the choice to bind themselves to Him?

6) In Egypt, Israel reached what is called the forty-ninth level of defilement, or *tumah*. (There are only fifty levels.) When *Hashem* took the Children of Israel out from under the hands of the Egyptians, He lifted them instantly from the depth of defilement and put them on the doorstep of the fiftieth gate of holiness — the highest level short of the

impossible-to-comprehend direct revelation of *Hashem* Himself.

If so, of course they accepted His offer. They had been covered with mud and then plucked out and given the cleanest, most regal of garments. Are they going to choose to go back into the mud? Is it a choice to throw off the clothes of royalty and return to desperate poverty? Since it is not, how does the decision of Israel to accept *Hashem*'s terms hold up?

The bottom line of all these questions is that, in one way or another, *Hashem* took away Israel's free will and forced them to accept His Torah, the instrument of unity. The question, then, is: If Israel's free will to accept the privilege and responsibility of being *Hashem*'s people was lacking in some fashion, then how could the marital bond have come to be?

The Long Chupah

The answer is: If the *chupah* had concluded at that time, and Israel been bound to *Hashem* based on that situation, then there would be reason to doubt the validity of the marital bond. However, Israel is still under the wedding canopy; the *chupah* is not finished. It is a long *chupah* which started at Sinai and will conclude with the coming of *Moshiach*.

A *chupah* ceremony today lasts little more than 15

minutes and is expected to produce a marital bond that lasts a few decades. If the marital bond is expected to last eternally, a 3,300-year *chupah* ceremony is not very long at all.

The underlying reason behind the length of the *chupah* is as follows: Both the *Chasan* (*Hashem*) and *kallah* (Israel) have to demonstrate their absolute willingness to become partners in the marriage. The *Chasan* has to demonstrate His willingness to marry this woman. The woman has to demonstrate her willingness to accept the Husband.

Therefore, the wedding is divided into two sections — one for the demonstration of the *Chasan*'s absolute love, and one for the demonstration of the *kallah*'s. And this, as we mentioned before, is the underlying idea behind the 2,000 years of Torah and the ensuing 2,000 years of the era of *yimos HaMoshiach*.

The first 2,000-year period represents the performance of the *Chasan*. The Torah is given — even "forced" upon us — through miracles and prophecy. Knowledge of *Hashem* is everpresent in an undeniable way. The power and beauty of the revelation of *Hashem*; the leadership of Moshe; the daily miracles in the *Bais HaMikdash*;[59] the words and deeds of the Prophets — *Hashem* gives, gives, gives. He shows He is willing to marry the *kallah* under any conditions — almost forcing Himself upon her. Under those circumstances, the *kallah* has no other choice but to receive.

The ensuing 2,000 year period — *yimos HaMoshiach* — are reserved for the performance of the *kallah*. The *kallah* must demonstrate what the *Chasan* demonstrated to her: that she wants Him under any circumstances, under any conditions. The emphasis switches from the giving of the Torah (*matan* Torah) to the receiving of the Torah (*kabbolas* HaTorah).

Therefore, the closer we are to the arrival of *Moshiach* the more darkness begins to engulf the Jewish people, the more *Hashem* withdraws His overt influence. The destruction of the *Bais HaMikdash*, the persecution of the Christians, the Crusades, the Black Plague, the Spanish Inquisition, the Cossack massacres, Shabbtai Zvi, the "Age of Enlightenment," the First World War, Communism, the Second World War, the Holocaust, the spiritual Holocaust[60] in America and Israel — this is the 2,000-year era of *Moshiach*, when the *Chasan* removes His influence, when He hides His face. It is our job — our opportunity — to find Him.

With this understanding, we are now ready to answer the six questions asked earlier. Each of the answers will reveal how the *Chasan* has taken away His overt influence in order to give the *kallah* Israel the opportunity to demonstrate her love. Each provides insight into six perplexing conditions which exist in the Jewish world, especially since the Holocaust:

1) The first question related to the fact that *Hashem*

held the mountain over the Jewish people. They were forced. They had no escape. It was like a *chasan* who said to his *kallah,* "I force you to marry me. I can't possibly be without you."

However, in order to counteract His influence, there must come a time when the *Chasan* seemingly lets His prospective *kallah* (Israel) go totally free. "If you don't want to be a Jew, don't be a Jew. Go out. Do anything you want."

All the acts of force, the imposition of conscience, of guilt, of society, of tradition — have to be totally, totally removed. Totally! *Hashem* will not stand in your way. In fact, just as there was force to be Jewish, there has to be a parallel time when Jews are forced not to be Jewish.

That state was accomplished perhaps nowhere more poignantly than in the Holocaust. To many Jews, the Holocaust signalled the end of their obligation to the *Chasan*. And so they abandoned Him. The repercussions are perhaps even more devastating. Jewish children are totally bereft of Torah knowledge. (Many may not even know that they are Jewish.) And this ignorance has resulted in the startling phenomenon that over 90 percent of Jews no longer observe Torah.

The perception that Jews are no longer obligated to keep Torah is part of the plan. It is the counterforce to the influences that had kept a large segment of Jewry within the Torah camp. Now, with those walls broken down, it is as if *Hashem* is saying, "Go. I do not hold the mountain over you any longer. If anything, I force you away."

2) As the Maharal explained, the mountain held over Israel's head was meant figuratively and was used to describe a positive force, a revelation of *Hashem* which left no room for denial. Therefore, in order to counteract that type of figurative force, there must be an equally strong figurative force that neutralizes the first. In the terminology of the Torah, this is called *hester panim*, the "hiding of the face [of *Hashem*]."[61] *Hester panim* is the opposite of revelation. *Hashem* hides so that even if one wants to see Him, he cannot.

The Jewish nation has undergone a particularly intense *hester panim* this century. "Where are You?" people ask. As the Torah predicts, they say, "Surely it is because our G-d is not in our midst that all these troubles have befallen us."[62]

3) The beauty of the *Chasan* blinded the *kallah* Israel. She became intoxicated with His "looks" and was carried away. In order to counteract that, there must come a time when *Hashem* does not appear beautiful. And that is the meaning of the words of the *Chasan* to the *kallah* in *Shir Hashirim*, "I am black. . ."[63] *Hashem* appears ugly. He is, in reality, no less beautiful than ever, however, on the surface

He will appear black, covered with soot. Nevertheless, His beauty is everpresent beneath the black exterior.

4) *Hashem* put Israel above nature; they became totally dependent upon Him for all their needs — shelter, food, water. There was no area where they exhibited independence. To counteract this, everything must be available without needing to turn to *Hashem*.

Communism attempted to demonstrate one's independence from *Hashem*. Unfortunately, Jews played a great part in bringing this ideology to the modern world. This is no coincidence. This idea was planted in them in order to counteract the influence of total reliance on *Hashem* in the desert. It is a counterforce to the idea that we are compelled to rely on *Hashem*.

In the West, a parallel phenomenon exists. Jews can be found in every field: business, politics, medicine. This situation differs drastically from the conditions endured in Europe for centuries and centuries. Today, it is relatively easy for everyone to make a living. If a Jew is successful, he makes it in business or in the professional world; and if he is not successful, he receives social services. Even the Jew in the Holy Land now has a government like any other.

In every way, privately and collectively, the Jew

appears self-sufficient. He has no need, it would seem, to turn to *Hashem* for sustenance. That, too, is part of the plan.

5) *Hashem* chose the nation of Israel; He isolated them in the desert and they became a "married woman." In opposition to this, there must come a time when the chosenness of Israel is rejected — even (and especially) by Jews. And that is, in fact, what we are witness to today. Many of those who most vehemently reject the idea of a chosen people are Jews. Of course, the baseless hatred of the non-Jew toward the Jew indicates that the Jews are different and chosen, yet the Jew has the most difficulty accepting *atoh bichartanu* — "You have chosen us."

Jews have complete freedom, and, superficially at least, total acceptance. They live a natural life dispersed among all the nations — not isolated — but assimilated. Now that they feel totally free and advocate equality for everyone, they have the choice to show if they are willing to be chosen, to show if they understand the meaning of being chosen. *Hashem* chose the Jews. Now, the Jewish people have to choose themselves.

6) At Mount Sinai, *Hashem* elevated the Jewish people to the highest level, to the doorstep of the "fiftieth gate of knowledge." Therefore, the reverse must, unfortunately, take place. There must come

> a time when *Hashem* causes the Jews to descend to the lowest level. This has been the case this century with forces such as the Holocaust, Communism, assimilation, and materialism. From each of these depths, Jews are challenged to elevate themselves — to show how much they really want the *Chasan*.

We should now have a clearer understanding of why the final generations before *Moshiach* are the most suffering, estranged generations. We do not see all the love and mercy of *Hashem*. If anything, the opposite appears — brutality, mercilessness, cruelty, silence. The inverse of what we experienced at the beginning of our nationhood has occurred because the *Chasan* is giving His *kallah* the opportunity to discover and announce her love for Him on her own.

While facing the exact same challenges, the final generation will be the diametric opposite of the generation that left Egypt. For instance, in Egypt all the devotion came from the side of the *Chasan*, from *Hashem*. *Hashem* struck the Egyptians; He split the Red Sea; He made Mount Sinai thunder, and spoke simultaneously to the millions of people. That was all His doing.

In the generation of *Moshiach*, the same devotion has to be demonstrated by the *kallah*. *Hashem* sits back — "hides" — and the Jewish people have to make the moves. We have to fight for the Torah. We have to fight to be Jewish. We have to break through all barriers to live up to the name Israel, the entity created to be *Hashem*'s partner.

The prophet Michah said: "Just as in the days when you went out of Egypt, the same wonders will recur in the end."[64] The same miracles, the same step-by-step development which took place at the inception of Israel's nationhood, will repeat themselves before *Moshiach* comes. However, it will occur in the opposite direction, and it will deliver a different message. For instance, the original splitting of the Red Sea revealed *Hashem*'s devotion. The equivalent to the splitting of the Red Sea, which will occur before the coming of *Moshiach*, will reveal the greatness of the *kallah*. Whereas Israel responded to the splitting sea with the statement, "This is my *Hashem*, and I will beautify Him,"[65] in the future, the *kallah* Israel will show such devotion that *Hashem* will say, "Who is like [My] people Israel?"[66]

The Breaking of the Glass

The *chupah* between *Hashem* and Israel began a little over 3,300 years ago and is still in progress. Our centuries of suffering are a tiny drop in the ocean of eternity. They are equivalent to that split-second pause the *kallah* may experience under the wedding canopy when she asks herself: "Do I really love him absolutely? Forever?" Then she pauses again and thinks: "I am crazy for even thinking that! Of course I love and adore him. I want him forever."

That "split-second pause" is a very painful, drawn-out process in the world of time. The Jewish people have been suffering many centuries. However, this lapse will pass. Eventually, the ceremony will be over and the marriage finalized.

How will we know when the ceremony is over?

Moshiach will arrive. Until he arrives, though, how can we know that the *chupah* is nearing its conclusion?

Probably the most well-known nuance of a Jewish wedding is the breaking of the glass. When the glass is broken, everyone screams, "Mazel tov!" The band starts to play, and the *kallah* and *chasan* are escorted down the aisle to the private room where the marriage is officially consummated. The breaking of the glass, then, signals the culmination of the wedding.

What does the breaking of the glass represent?

It represents the destruction of the *Bais HaMikdash*.[67] Therefore, before *Moshiach* comes, the last generation will reexperience destruction equivalent to the breaking of the glass.

In Nazi Germany, the reality of the impending Holocaust was foreshadowed by the night now infamously referred to as Krystalnacht, the night of shattered glass. The tragedy of that night needs no elaboration. However, the potential blessing of that night needs a great deal of explanation. The Holocaust, the post-Holocaust wars and sufferings, as well as the personal holocausts of every individual, are all in fact answers to the question:

Are we nearing the end of our test? The answer is: Yes! The time to shout, "Mazel tov!" is upon us.

> *K'doshim t'hiyu kee kodosh ani Hashem Elokeichem*, "You shall be holy because I, *Hashem* your G-d, am holy." (Vayikra 19:2)
> *Kadaish atzmicha b'mutar loch*, "Sanctify yourself with that which is permissible to you." (Ramban)

When a person is in pain, he is likely to feel that he has no obligation to anyone or anything. All that matters is the pain. When it seems like we have no obligation to uphold the Torah — when we are experiencing the broken glass of holocaust, private or communal — that is the time to accept *Hashem*'s offer of Torah as never before. That is the time to sanctify ourselves, to turn ourselves into holy beings who radiate an other-worldly transcendance.

The giving of the Torah on Mount Sinai was not a one-time occurrence. *Hashem* is extending His hand and offering us the Torah even now. (That is why we conclude the blessing over learning Torah *nosain HaTorah*, *Hashem* Who "is *giving* the Torah," not merely *Hashem* Who *gave* Torah once in the past.) Torah, the wedding ring, is still being offered. However, we have to take it.

The time when one's life seems shattered like broken glass is a time ripe with blessing. It is the time when one has the opportunity to express a love and devotion to *Hashem* that is neither dependent on rewards nor beclouded by extraneous stimulants. Of course, to be able to shout "Mazel tov!" during adversity requires a presence of mind that soars above and beyond normal human nature. But that is what Jews are all about: towering above and beyond normal human nature and events. How else could we have picked up the pieces and outlived our oppressors all these centuries?

How does one acquire that presence of mind? Through knowledge. Through understanding the purpose of suffering.

We shout "Mazel Tov!" during the glass breaking at a Jewish wedding because we understand that it is part of a larger event — the joyous occasion called marriage. If not for that larger context, something like the breaking of the glass would be an intrusion on that joy. However, Jewish people have conditioned themselves to shout "Mazel Tov!" so much over the centuries that the moment the breaking of the glass has become associated with the peak of joy.

The same is true in a figurative sense. The 2,000-year period of Jewish suffering is a drop in the ocean of eternity and just one part of a much greater event — the wedding between *Hashem* and Israel. A Jew, who composes the entity Israel, has every reason to shout "Mazel Tov!" especially during a Krystalnacht because, in the greater context, it signifies the approaching climax of the most joyous occasion. And although accepting suffering with love requires great presence of mind, it breeds a love of *Hashem* which is absolute, a love which is not possible to achieve without the suffering. That awareness makes the shouts of "Mazel Tov!" all the more meaningful. Thus, there is no moment more pregnant with blessing than the moment we experience a Krystalnacht, personal or communal. (See also Question 12 in the Appendix.)

Doing It to Ourselves

As we have said, the past centuries have witnessed an ever-deepening *hester panim*, hiding of *Hashem*'s face. It is important to note the transition from a nation privy to miracles and prophecy into a scattered people persecuted and degraded in the eyes of the world was also brought about by our own doing. In other words, not only did *Hashem* hide and remove His Presence — we chased Him away.

This is perhaps best symbolized with the death of Zechariah the prophet. Zechariah ben Yehoyoda was killed by Jews because he warned them that they would lose the *Bais HaMikdash* if they persisted in their ways. They responded by killing Zechariah — in the *Bais HaMikdash*, no less.

How could Jews do this?

On one level, we can understand it drawing from the fact that Jews are born human. *Hashem* gave Israel the Torah to help them fulfill their potential to be more than human. (And anyone who sincerely scrutinizes the history of Israel will discern the superior spiritual and moral accomplishments of the Jewish people.) But, after all, Jews are made of flesh and blood. Their human imperfections produced a situation where desire for forbidden relations, idol worship, and bloodshed infiltrated their society. (Yet, even then, their overall society was far superior to the immorality and brutality of today's "civilized" world.) That much we can understand.

The question remains, however, how did a people distinguished from the rest of mankind by *Hashem* even have the possibility of sinking so low? *Hashem* took them out of Egypt miraculously and gave them the Torah. Theoretically, that should have enabled them to rise until they all literally resembled angels. Yet, that did not happen. Was there some specific initial character flaw hidden within them? Or was it something outside of them? Or was it perhaps a combination of these two factors?

The key to resolving this question lies in what we have explained previously: a platform for the *kallah* — a "new order" — had to come into existence at some point. *Hashem* intended to give His people the free will to show their love for Him, independent of His input. He tested them. If Israel had passed the test, the entire history of Jewish suffering and exile would not have been necessary.

What was the test?

Moshe delayed returning from the mountain with the

tablets of the ten commandments.

Chazal tell us that the angel of evil tested the people severely and led them to believe Moshe had died.[68] As a result, a small minority of the lower elements of the people were able to lead others into making the Golden Calf. *That failed test at the beginning of Israel's formation, became the seed of all the later problems.* It manifested itself in the people as an excessively strong desire to rebel, giving them the ability to appear as if they were purposely trying to destroy their special relationship with *Hashem*.

The same situation occurred with Adam, the first man. How did Adam have the power to sin while living in the Garden of Eden with the Presence of *Hashem* around him (equivalent to the revelation at Mount Sinai)? The answer is that his devotion to *Hashem*'s word was also tested. He, too, failed the test.

The Purpose of Chutzpah

We have to further understand the source of this will to rebel.

Hashem created human beings with a great need to rebel. If there was no ability to resist the influences of society, ideology, parents, teachers, etc. then one could never become an independent person. In order to become you — in order to exercise your freedom — you must be able to rebel. The tendency to rebel is a sign of an entity exercising free choice.

Thus, *chutzpah* is very important to the human psyche. It gives us the ability to rebel. Without *chutzpah* we would be robots. *Hashem* gave us free choice so that we could be whatever we want to be, not what the established culture (or counter-culture) wants us to be.

But why give us free choice when it can literally destroy us? It is good to let us know that we have the potential to destroy ourselves. However, what good does it do if we actually go ahead and destroy ourselves?

The answer is that we can never fully destroy ourselves. Evil is a temporary creation meant to be phased out after its purpose is completed.[69] Good, which is everlasting, must ultimately triumph. Furthermore, we can never fully destroy ourselves because Israel is eternal. This is a promise *Hashem* gave the forefathers. A generation can destroy itself, but the next generation will have the ability to rebuild. In the larger picture, eternity is guaranteed.[70]

Of course, the question still applies: Why did the destruction come through Israel's own hands? The answer is: *so Israel would know that the reconstruction could come through their own hands as well.*

Hashem can always tell Israel: If you were strong enough to violate Me in the Garden of Eden, to make a Golden Calf 40 days after the revelation on Mount Sinai, worship idols in the time of the *Bais HaMikdash*, and kill Zechariah the prophet, then why aren't you strong enough to violate the anti-Torah influences which hold you in their grasps? The same *chutzpah* you employed to destroy your spiritual stature can be used to rebuild it.

Because of "our" sins, we were thrown out of the land. So, too, because of "our" *teshuva* we will merit returning to the land. We shouldn't wait for Him to make us do *teshuva.* We have to bring ourselves back. We have to discover Him in Auschwitz or in the spiritual wastelands of America and Israel. And when we do, we become a full partner with *Hashem* in the rebuilding of the world.

Wrestling With Hashem

This idea is illustrated magnificently by *Chazal:*[71]

> The *luchos,* the tablets on which the ten commandments were written, were six *tefachim* in length (one *tefach* equals a handsbreadth). When Moshe went up into heaven to receive them, two *tefachim* were held by *Hashem*, two *tefachim* by Moshe, and two *tefachim* between them were unheld. At the very moment when Moshe and *Hashem* simultaneously held onto the tablets, the Jewish people were committing the sin of worshipping the Golden Calf. *Hashem* wanted to grab the tablets from Moshe. However, Moshe did not let Him. They struggled. Moshe overpowered *Hashem* and grabbed them away. He brought them down to the people at Mount Sinai and broke them. *Hashem* told Moshe, "Thank you for breaking them."

Every statement by *Chazal* is a meaning-packed message. They are communicating profound truths in the garb of mundane or seemingly far-flung symbols.

Many questions are raised by the above passage. How can man fight with *Hashem*? More importantly, how can he win the fight? Think about the power struggle. It is understandable that *Hashem* wanted to take the tablets away. After all, the Jewish people were sinning with the Golden Calf. Why, though, did Moshe want to grab them back?

Picture it this way: The *chasan* is standing underneath the *chupah* giving the ring to the *kallah*. She has barely slipped her finger into the ring when, suddenly, she spits in his face. At that moment, the *chasan* is thinking: "What *chutzpah*! I can't marry such a person! The marriage is not yet final. I am still holding the ring."

He begins to pull the ring back. However, the *kallah* twists her finger and does not let him pull it off. A power struggle ensues between them. Eventually, she wins. Then she tells him, "Too bad for you. Now we are married. You are stuck with me." And then she goes and breaks the ring.

That is similar to the scenario *Chazal* paint for us. We can understand why *Hashem* would want to take away the tablets. Why, though, was Moshe fighting? To bring them down to people who were not ready for them? As it was, when he returned and saw the Golden Calf, he broke the tablets anyway. And even if there is some explanation, why would *Hashem* thank Moshe for breaking them? These questions beg for answers.

Absolute Free Choice

The underlying idea can be explained using the theme of *Hashem* and Israel as marriage partners. *Chazal* tell us: *ishto k'gufo*, a man's wife is like himself. If so, and if, as we have been saying, Israel is the *kallah* of *Hashem*, then what exactly does it mean that Israel, the *kallah*, is like *Hashem*?

Man was created *b'tzelem Elokim*,[72] in the image of *Hashem*. *Hashem* is absolutely unbound to anything else. He is one, He is alone. Thus, it can be said, among other things, that *Hashem* has absolute free choice. Nothing sways Him to go one way or the other. Absolutely nothing. If we are made in the image of *Hashem*, then, among other things, it must mean that we have absolute free choice. Nothing can sway us one way or the other.

Now, imagine a king who marries a very simple woman. He tells her that when she becomes queen, she will have the same power as he. She will be able to do anything she wants. That is the idea of *ishto k'gufo*, a man's wife is like himself.

Picture this queen saying, "I can't wait to test my power. If I am really going to be as powerful as him, then let me spit in his face as we get married, right under the *chupah*. If I can do anything I want, then I can even rebel against *him*."

Why would she rebel immediately, underneath the wedding canopy? Why wouldn't she wait until later?

The reason is because her power at that moment will

never be equalled. The first instant of marriage possesses a unity greater than at any other time. The moment the man gives the woman the ring, their desire for each other is at its peak. The full potential of unity — of *yichud* — exists at the moment of the giving of the ring.

Love and hate are, often, opposite sides of the same coin. When deep love does not find expression in a positive way, it usually finds expression as hatred. One has to learn how to channel emotions in the right way. If the moment of great unity is not used positively, it is bound to be used in the opposite way.

The climax of unity between *Hashem* and Israel was the short moment when Moshe and *Hashem* held onto the tablets, as the Jews stood perched at the foot of Mount Sinai. That moment possessed the absolute potential for *yichud*, the absolute potential for unity. However, the people had not yet learned how to use that potential positively. They, therefore, abused the power and made the Golden Calf.

At Mount Sinai, the nation of Israel wanted to test the extent of their free choice, to see just how far being created in *Hashem's* image went. They wondered: Would their free choice even make them free of *Hashem*? The answer was: Yes. You can make the Golden Calf. You can kill My prophets. You can violate My Torah. You have that power.

Didn't *Hashem* know what would happen? What could possibly be gained by allowing the people to build the

Golden Calf, by allowing the "*kallah*" to spit in the "*Chasan*'s" face?

The answer may by now appear familiar: If you have the ability to use your free choice to make a Golden Calf, kill a prophet, and cause the tablets containing the ten commandments to be broken — things which are against *Hashem*'s wishes — recognize the power you have to make yourselves heroes, prophets, and sages who recapture Torah. No power in the world — not even *Hashem* Himself! — can take Torah, the unifying force between *Hashem* and Israel, away from the Jew. Even if you are as great a heretic as Achair (Elisha ben Avuyah) who heard a heavenly voice proclaim, "Return, My children, return. Everyone can do *teshuva* except Achair"[73] you can do *teshuva.* Although Achair did indeed hear that heavenly voice, the commentators explain that he should have realized that even he had the power to negate the heavenly decree against him and return to Torah ways.

In fact, if you want to measure your potential for strength, know that Moshe overpowered *Hashem.* He wrestled with Him and grabbed away the tablets at the moment of greatest unity with sheer willpower. Thus, you too can overcome all adversity — even adversity orchestrated by *Hashem.* Grab onto your own *luchos.* That is the lesson of this beautiful passage from *Chazal.*

Thank You for Breaking the Tablets

With these insights, we can answer why Moshe broke the tablets and why *Hashem* thanked him for doing so.

There were two sets of tablets. The first set was made by *Hashem* and inscribed by *Hashem*. This set was broken by Moshe. The second set, although *inscribed* by *Hashem* like the first, was *carved* out of rock by Moshe. Only regarding the second set does the Torah say: *p'sal lecha*, "carve out for yourself."[74]

The first set of tablets represents the first 2,000-year period, *matan* Torah, the giving of Torah. The second 2,000-year period, *yimos HaMoshiach*, is represented by the second set of tablets, *kabbolas* HaTorah. *Hashem* thanked Moshe for breaking the first set because he created the possibility for the *kallah* Israel to perform her part in the marriage, to do her share, which involved making the second set of tablets. Without that, the marriage would have been one-sided. When a marriage is one-sided, even (and especially) when that one side is as perfect as *Hashem*, the other side feels lacking. Moshe broke the first set of tablets in order to be able to create a two-sided marriage, a unity not only from *chasan* to *kallah* but of *kallah* to *chasan*. That is why *Hashem* said, "Thank you."

CHAPTER 5

THE HOLOCAUST

Now that we have laid out a framework for understanding the history of Jewish suffering, I want to relate a few stories and then describe how they fit into that framework. The first story is one I heard from my rebbi and mentor, Rabbi Michoel Dov Weissmandel *zt'l*.

German decimation of a Jewish community began with deportation. Armed soldiers would wake up defenseless and unprepared Jews in the middle of the night, chase them out of their homes, and congregate them in the center of the city, the *umschlagplatz*. From there they would take them to the train station and squeeze 80 or 90 people into a cattle car with space for no more than 20 or 30 people. They would lock the door and deprive them of food.

Many times, it took a day or two before the train received clearance to depart. Delays were especially common toward the end, in 1944, when the last million Jews from Czechoslovakia and Hungary were deported to Auschwitz.

That is the way it happened during the final liquidation of the city of Nitra, Czechoslovakia — Rabbi Weissmandel's home town. The Germans chased the Jews out of their homes early in the morning and jammed them into the cattle cars. Whole families — fathers, mothers, and little children — were packed together so tightly it was impossible to even sit. As they stood for a day or more the sun burned mercilessly over their heads. The children asked and begged for food and water, but there was nothing to give them. It was in situations like this, that the true character of *om Yisroel*, the people of Israel, could be found.

A story Rabbi Weissmandel repeated many times concerned a chicken farmer. This simple Jew was powerless to help his family members, who were suffering enormously like everyone else. But when he looked out from a small window and saw a Jew free on the streets (the Germans allowed certain Jewish craftsmen free until they had no further need for them) he screamed out, "Yankel, do me a favor. Go to my house and feed my chickens. Remember, *tsaar baalay chaim, di'Oraysoh*, 'to inflict pain on animals is forbidden Biblically.'"

Here was a man stripped entirely of his humanity. His own family was dying in front of him. He was not obligated to worry about his chickens. In fact, he could very easily have lifted his eyes to heaven and said, "Master of the Universe, where is Your commitment toward keeping *tsaar baalay chaim*? If we were not good enough as Jews, at least take care of us as animals and see that we shouldn't suffer. And, if I'm not even worthy as an animal, why do my children have to suffer so much? They ask for water and food, but I have nothing to give them."

Was this Jew obligated, under such conditions, to care about the pain of the chickens? Of course not. Yet, his devotion to *Hashem*'s Torah, even under the most inhumane conditions, was second nature. He was saying in effect, "*Hashem*, I will not let You grab the Torah from me. I wrestle with You even now to possess it on my own."

This is the story of a simple farmer. Of course, there are many comparable stories about great rabbis and well-known leaders. Rabbi Weissmandel liked to tell this particular story, though, because it showed how even the simple Jew could prove "Who is like Your people Israel?"

Another story concerns a mother who had just arrived at a concentration camp. Knowing she would soon be separated from her newborn, she yelled, "I will not depart from my little child unless someone first gives me a knife."

Her friends tried to dissuade her from taking the knife to the child. In the midst of the commotion, though, a German soldier came over. Asking about the source of the commotion, he was told that the woman wanted a knife "before parting from her child." With typical German sadism, the Nazi took his knife and "generously" gave it to the woman.

Taking the knife, the woman put the baby on the ground. She raised the knife . . . and performed *bris milah*, a circumcision on the infant.

Her one concern, her last wish, was that her child have a proper *bris* on this his eight day of life. When she finished, her face radiated joy. She handed the knife and the child over to the German, and said, "*Hashem* gave me a healthy baby. I am returning a Jewish baby to Him."

This woman was in no way obligated to fulfill the commandment of *bris milah* under such circumstances. Yet, it was her one wish. What did her act show? It was the performance of the *kallah*. "*Hashem,* we love you," she was saying. "We love Your Torah, the ring that signifies our engagement to You. Just as You accepted us under all circumstances in Egypt, we accept You under all circumstances, no matter how much You hide Your presence."

Perhaps even greater testimony of the legacy of Jewish devotion can be seen in the stories of Jewish children.

Let me share some of them with you.

In the month of Nissan 5704 (1944) a doctor came to talk to approximately 200 Jewish Hungarian boys deported to a concentration camp. He told them, "As you know, the Germans are killing Jews every day. First, they make them work until they have no strength left. Then, when they are too weak to be of any further use, they are sent to the gas chambers.

"However," he continued, "the benevolent Prince Primac, of Hungary, has announced that the Christian Church wants to save Jews. The Church will assure the safety of any Jew willing to baptize himself."

When not one boy responded, the doctor continued: "Why should you face such an unbearably hopeless situation? I will give you three days to think it over. Anyone who comes forward and is willing to be baptized will be protected by the Church."

When the doctor left the room, the children immediately burst out, "*Rasha*! Wick one!" they said in disgust. "The good Christians talk of love and shelter, but they will not accept you unless you become one of them."

Three days later, the doctor returned and not one boy came forward to take his offer.

There is another well-known story about the loyalty of Jewish children. The famous Cracow Bais Yaakov Seminary for Girls, founded by Sarah Shenirer, attracted girls from across Europe. Since many of the girls were from out of town they were unable to return home when the war broke out. They remained there day after day, week after week, until it became obvious that the war was going to prevent them from returning home for quite some time.

The teachers gave them encouragement and tactfully prepared them for the worst: how to die *ahl kiddush Hashem* (sanctifying G-d's name), if need be. On the twelfth day of the month of Av (around August) 5702 (1942), the principal made a speech to the 93 young women who remained.

"Dear daughters," she began, "we ask *Hashem* every day not to test us. And if He should give us a test, we ask Him to give us the courage and strength to withstand the test. We are living in a very difficult time. We have to remember the words Moshe spoke to us: '*HaTzur tomim poalo*, [*Hashem*] is a Rock; all His actions are pure. He is righteous and absolutely just.'[75] The time may come when you will be called upon to demonstrate everything you have learned. You have to show how Jewish children are loyal to *Hashem* and how they can withstand all kinds of tests."

A few days later, some gestapo agents entered the dormitory of this Bais Yaakov Seminary. They ordered the girls to go to the public bathhouse and then dress in their best clothes. Then they told the principal, "Tomorrow, 93 gestapo men will come here and each one will take a girl as an escort. The girls do not have to fear that we will hurt them. We just want some entertainment."

When the principal heard that, she knew the test was upon them. She allowed the girls to bathe and dress up. Before the gestapo showed up, though, she called the girls together and told them, "Dear children, I know that all of you are prepared to give up your lives for *Hashem*, if it has to be so. And I know that you are ready to accept serenely any torture which maybe meted out to you. However, these gestapo monsters have even more diabolical plans. They are not merely seeking to destroy us physically, but to first do so spiritually."

The young women who listened to the words of their principal became petrified with fear. Sensing this, the principal told them, "I have prepared for this occasion." She paused and then said, "I have poison tablets for all of us. If it should come to the point that any one of them wants to touch you, take the tablet. Never let them besmirch your soul."

After the initial shock, the girls felt electrified with inner strength. Their faces radiated confidence and contentment. One by one, each girl stepped forward and took a poison tablet from the principal.

The following day, just as the gestapo agents arrived, the girls congregated in the assembly room and said the preliminary blessing, "We are prepared to perform the commandment of dying *ahl kiddush Hashem*."

Then, together, each of them swallowed the tablet. They did not wait for the gestapo. The principal took her tablet and said, "Let us together, one last time, shout the words a Jew says before she dies, *Shma Yisroel . . .* "

They said the *Shma* and its ensuing verses until, one by one, each of them passed from this world.

The Point: Spiritual Resistance

The Holocaust is an unspeakable tragedy. However, it is a pointless tragedy if we do not at least learn the lessons it was meant to teach us: the most noble resistance Jews offered in the Holocaust was spiritual resistance. And this kind of resistance, Jews undertook again and again.

Unfortunately, this fact is almost always lost on the non-Torah historian or the layman who dabbles in popular Holocaust literature. While the average person may understand the resistance of the Warsaw Ghetto uprising or the Jewish partisans who fought with the underground, military reprisal and resistance represent only one type of Jewish response in the Holocaust — and not even the most common or significant kind.

The primary and most noble resistance Jews offered in the Holocaust was spiritual resistance. They did not allow the Nazis to strip them of their identity — and destruction of Jewish identity was exactly what the Nazis were after. They did not merely seek to destroy the Jewish body, they wanted the Jewish soul.

On the festival of *Simchas Torah*, a large group of Jewish boys, no more than 15 or 16 years of age, were brought out of their barracks to be sent to the gas chambers. One of them spoke up and said, "Today is *Simchas Torah*, the day we are supposed to rejoice with the Torah. Let us take one last dance with the Torah in absolute joy."

"But we have no Torah scroll," another one said.

"But *Hashem* is with us," he replied.

They started dancing and singing like never before. The Nazis were beside themselves.

"Why are you dancing?" they asked.

"Because it is *Simchas Torah*; we are rejoicing with *Hashem*; He gave us the Torah; He made us Jews; He gave us eternal life."

"Don't you know what is about to happen to you?" the Nazis asked.

"Yes, but we are not going to die now; you are only moving us from the material world to the spiritual world; we are going to meet our parents whom you killed yesterday; you can't really kill us."

The Nazis were so maddened by this that they returned the children to their barracks.

If the Nazis just wanted to exterminate Jews, what difference did it make what the children did before they killed them? The answer is that Hitler and his henchmen were not content to simply kill all the Jews; they wanted to break the Jewish spirit because nothing opposed what they represented more.

What exactly did the Jew represent to the Nazi?

To get to the root of that question, you have to know that the Holocaust was simply the playing out of a scenario which has repeated itself many times throughout history. It is the scenario of the struggle between Yaakov and Esav.

In Torah terminology, Yaakov is the pure spiritual ideal, the spark of eternity. His twin brother, Esav, personifies materialism, the ideal of experiencing the material life as an end in itself.[76]

Esav was born with a strong materialistic nature, but had the free will to align himself with Yaakov, thereby effecting a unity of the spiritual and material that would have given even Esav a share in eternity. Instead of joining Yaakov, however, Esav persisted in his pursuit of the material, and deepened his hatred for Yaakov and everything he represented.

Esav's refusal to pursue his brother's ideals is the root of anti-semitism.[77] *Hashem* gave all mankind an opportunity to gain immortality. However, only the forefathers pursued absolute righteousness and earned the title Israel, thereby securing eternity as a genuine possession for themselves and their offspring.[78] No one could possibly have felt the failure of that lost opportunity more intensely than Esav, the offspring of Avraham and Yitzchak. Rather than changing his ways, he deepened his indulgence and convinced others, who might otherwise have attached themselves to Yaakov, to partake in his hatred.

Esav's greatest "success" in this regard was his grandchild Amalek, whose hatred was so fanatical that his descendants sacrificed everything in a vain attempt to destroy the Children of Israel (Yaakov) in the desert after they were miraculously taken out of Egypt. While unsuccessful, he succeeded in injecting his venomous, baseless hatred into others. That venom runs through the veins of society today.

Hitler was the modern day Amalek. His fanatical hatred was based on a deep-seated lust for power and possession. It went so far, in fact, that he was not merely interested in short-term power or partial possession; he wanted materialism which was to be the vaunted "thousand-year Reich." He wanted immortality, the ultimate possession.

In essence, Hitler, the modern Amalek, envied the Jewish (Yaakov's) spark of eternity.[79] The persecuted, exiled, and perpetually wandering Jew, if for no other reason than the mere fact of his existence, laid a claim to eternity that had to arouse Hitler's envy. The Jewish people defied all the rules of history. In his own mind, they represented a claim on immortality that threatened his own designs. Therefore, he wanted a "New Order;" he, Esav/Amalek, wanted to topple the "Old Order" where Yaakov was on top.

Was Hitler really aware of his part in the ongoing saga of Yaakov versus Esav/Amalek?

His writings reveal that he was aware of quite a lot. As

he blamed the Jews for all of society's evils, he revealed the extent to which he believed the Jews were responsible for the world in which he found himself. In his distorted mind, he envisioned his Third Reich as the civilization which would supplant the civilization Jews had built.

Esav and his by-products represent the drive for materialism which seeks independence from spiritual and moral responsibility. Hitler understood that Judaism was the foundation of modern moral consciousness. As indicated in his writings, he was obsessed with denying Judaism so that the world's material urges could be freed of Jewish conscience. Therefore, before exterminating Jews, whenever he could, Hitler tried to oppress and degrade the Jew. By doing so, he hoped to physically and spiritually rid the world of the Jewish presence because, as he saw it, Jews were the real obstacle to the emergence of an immortal Third Reich. And, in a way, he was correct in that assessment, because the Torah teaches us that it is the Jewish people who are destined to build the eternal Third Temple.

When those children danced because they were Jews — and because Jews dance on *Simchas Torah* — the Nazis in attendance saw their thousand-year Reich teeter; their belief in their own immortality was shaken to the foundation. Here was palpable evidence of a people who, despite their imprisoned, degraded, and hopeless state, exuded a confidence and belief in immortality which shattered their own. In many ways, they toppled the Third Reich before the Allied soldiers.

At first glance, Hitler appears more successful than Amalek. However, in reality, his failure further compounds the evidence that indeed there is an eternal people walking on this temporary earth.

The legacy of simple Jews and learned Jews, Jewish men and Jewish women, Jewish adults and Jewish children, Jews of every walk of life and background — all demonstrating absolute loyalty to Torah — is part of a historical tapestry spanning numerous centuries. All told, it is a loud and clear declaration stating, in effect, "We are not restricted to the temporary world. And we are willing to prove that fact by sacrificing everything of the temporal world so that we can be Your partner *Hashem* in the eternal world."

It is a spiritual crime, and an injustice to those who perished in the Holocaust, to view Jewish suffering without placing it against the backdrop of everything the Jewish people have strived for for over three millennia. Jewish history — and especially the history of Jewish suffering — is a testing ground of Jewish devotion to the eternal values of the Torah. The Holocaust is the most recent, and in many ways the most difficult of these tests, but it too has its place. Despite the utter hopelessness of their situation, the heroes enumerated in this small sampling of stories did not lose sight of the fact that a Jew's mission in this world is to serve *Hashem* with absolute devotion. The Nazi? He was just a temporary flash in the pan of history. For a time he held power. However, soon he too would pass. All that would remain of significance was the amount of Jewish devotion to *Hashem* and Torah each Jew had shown in the face of such evil.

The Holocaust, like the entire history of Jewish suffering (and like every private experience of suffering), has to be viewed through the lens of Torah. That, in and of itself, is the beginning of the redemptive process.

More Stories Within Our Framework

Let us return momentarily to the conceptual framework of Jewish history enumerated near the end of the last chapter and view a few more stories in that light.

In the last chapter, we elaborated on the *Midrash* which depicted how Moshe wrestled with *Hashem* to hold onto the tablets of the ten commandments (the *luchos*). We explained that it symbolized no power in the universe (not even *Hashem*!) could take Torah away from the Jew if the Jew did not allow it. Where have we witnessed this ability a Jew has to overpower *Hashem* as Moshe did?

In the Holocaust.

In the ghettos of Nazi-occupied Europe, there was an underground group of yeshiva youth whose founder was a young man called Mattisyahu. Born into an assimilated Viennese family, Mattisyahu became a deeply committed

Torah Jew, a *baal teshuva,* by age 15 — despite the fervent opposition of his father. He eventually left home and came to Poland, where he entered a yeshiva and quickly developed into a budding scholar.

By the time the Germans occupied Poland he had become the leader of a group of young men fervently devoted to Torah ideals. The Germans decreed that all Jewish men had to shave their beards and *peyos*. Jews had to work on *Shabbos* if they were to get ration cards to buy bread. Mattisyahu told his group that it was a *gezeras haShmad*, an attempt to get Jews to deny their religion.

"You can be sure," he said, "that they intend to kill all the Jews eventually. This is an attempt to take our souls before they take our bodies. We are not going to give in to their demands. We will go underground. We are going to keep our beards and *peyos,* observe *Shabbos,* and learn Torah until we die. We will dedicate ourselves to serving *Hashem* fully with the last days of our lives."

They went into hiding. The community secretly supported them with the little food they had, and came to view these young men as a source of pride. Other groups of young men in other ghettos modeled themselves after them. And these groups, wherever they cropped up, were invariably the last Jews to survive, going to their death with their holy books in their hands and with "*Shma Yisroel. . .*" on their lips.

A diary of one of the last survivors of Mattisyahu's

groups was discovered. He describes how he is the last one left in his bunker. Dying of starvation and experiencing tortuous suffering, he writes how he knows that within a couple of hours the fires raging about him will end his life. He knows, according to Jewish law, he is allowed to jump into the fire. Nevertheless, he debates with himself whether to jump into the fire and shorten his hours of pain or to stay alive until the fires burn him up. As he writes, he is reminded of a story about the plight of a Jew during the Spanish Inquisition.

The Marranos were Spanish Jews who converted to Christianity under threat of death but secretly maintained Jewish law and custom — despite the risk of getting burned at the stake if they were discovered. As the story goes, one aristocratic Marrano family was discovered. Forewarned by a friend that the authorities were coming to get them, they managed to flee, albeit emptyhanded and barefooted. They wandered for weeks and weeks until they finally found their way to a refugee camp in Morocco. Conditions there were dire and impoverished — certainly a far cry from the aristocratic lifestyle they were used to — but at least they were with others like themselves.

Then plague struck the camp. Death hung everywhere. One morning, a child of this Marrano family did not wake up. Shortly thereafter, another child died. Soon, all the children died. The parents remained as strong as they could and accepted their fate. Then, finally, the wife died.

When that happened, the husband lifted his eyes to heaven and said, "*Hashem*, I know that everything has been a challenge to see if I would stop believing in You and loving You, to see if I would break. What is left for You to try to break me with?

"When they forced us to feign Christianity. We remained dedicated to Your Torah in private. We lived under constant fear of being caught and that did not deter us. Then we had the choice to accept death or flee in order to continue living. We fled. And then you took away one child. We did not complain. And then You took our next child. And still we accepted Your decree. Eventually, You took all the children. And now You have taken away my wife. What else is there for You to break me with?

"As I see it," he exclaimed, "there are only two things left. One is my life and the other is my belief in You. If you want to take away my life, go ahead and take it. It is not mine to begin with; it is Yours. However, if you want to take away my belief in and love for You — that, even You, Almighty, cannot take away. They belong to me — and to me alone."

Now, in the bunker in one of the burning Jewish ghettos of Nazi-occupied Europe, this starved, tortured young Jew recalled the story of the Marrano. He wrote: "When I reminded myself of this story, I reminded myself that these moments of 'confrontation' with

Hashem are the most precious moments a person can possess because they allow one to prove absolute love of and devotion to *Hashem*." It was then that he decided not to jump into the flames prematurely. He turned to *Hashem*: "In these moments, when there is no hope, and no apparent reason or purpose to live, I know that everything You have done is a test to see if we still love You, to see if we still want Your Torah and *mitzvos*, if we still believe in You. You fought us. You fought me. But You did not break me. Soon I am going to be consumed by fire. But I will not rush to my death. These last few painful hours You have given me do indeed contain a purpose: to prove to You that even if the life You have given becomes a living hell, it is still the most precious possession because we can use it to tell You that You cannot stop us from loving You. You can take our lives, but not our desire for You. You can test us with anything You like; I promise that I will fight You to the last moment."

Sometimes, it seems like *Hashem* is fighting us. We want to be good Jews and serve Him and keep His Torah, but everything seems to be working against us. However, we should never despair. *Hashem* may be engaging us — challenging us — but He does so in order for us to discover the lesson that no power can take away our ability to love Him.

In a chess match, each player makes moves and counter-moves, hiding from his opponent, as best he can, the strategy behind each move. Life is like a chess match where *Hashem* makes moves we are expected to react to. We, in turn, make moves which He reacts to. Our challenge is to figure out the intention behind His moves and counter them. When two people play chess, normally each of them wants to win. However, when a father and a son play, if the son outsmarts the father and wins, the father receives more enjoyment than had he won himself. Similarly, when we defeat *Hashem* in this fashion, He, too, has more pleasure.

This is the understanding behind an otherwise cryptic statement the *Gemara* attributed to *Hashem*, namely: *nitzchunie bohni*, "My children have defeated Me."[80] The sages, Rabbi Yehoshua and Rabbi Eliezer, had a disagreement. The latter kept invoking miraculous signs to substantiate his opinion, so much so that he finally said, "Let a voice come from heaven proving I am right." The heavenly voice indeed came and substantiated his opinion. To this, however, Rabbi Yehoshua countered with a direct quote from the Torah, "It [the Torah] is not in heaven."[81] *Hashem* said in regard to Rabbi Yehoshua's response, "*nitzchunie bohni.*" In other words, the truth of the response was so clever that even the heavenly voice was conclusively countered.

Of course, man cannot normally outsmart *Hashem*. Nevertheless, when *Hashem* really wants to "lose," then it is within the power of a person to dig deep within himself and use every resource he has to "outsmart"

Hashem. That is what Rabbi Yehoshua did. That is also a way to understand the response of Jews in the Holocaust.

For instance, when *Pesach* came many Jews, even in the worst concentration camps, tried their best to obtain *matzah*. However, it was not always possible. When it became apparent to these dying, starved Jews that they would not be able to eat *matzah*, their hearts were even more broken than their bodies. Under those life and death conditions, a Jew is allowed, even obligated, to eat anything in order to keep himself alive — even if the only thing to eat is *chometz*, otherwise absolutely forbidden to eat during Passover.

In one camp, a group of Jews decided not to despair. They were going to make a Passover *Seder* using bread. They quietly congregated and recited the *Hagadah* from memory, telling all the stories of the exodus from Egypt. As it came time to eat the *matzah*, they took the bread and composed a prayer: "Master of the Universe, You know very well that our desire is really to fulfill the commandment required for tonight, that is, to eat *matzah*. However, You have not given us the opportunity to eat *matzah*. Not only do You not allow us to perform the commandment of eating *matzah*, but You are also compelling us to eat *chometz*. Otherwise we will perish. Even though we cannot fulfill the commandment of eating *matzah*, we are going to fulfill an even greater commandment: preserving life. And, therefore, with the intention of fulfilling the great commandment of preserving our lives, we make the blessing *hamotzi lechem min ha'aretz*, 'He who brings forth bread from the earth.'"

They closed their eyes and ate the *chometz* as if it was the most precious *mitzvah.* We can imagine how, at that moment, *Hashem* looked down upon them from heaven and said with pride, *nitzchunie bohni*, "My children have defeated Me . . . I took away their ability to perform the *mitzvah* of eating *matzah.* But they replaced it with an even greater *mitzvah* — preserving life. They have 'outsmarted' Me."

We never need consider our situation hopeless. We are capable, under any conditions, during the most unbearable, torturous moments, of proving to *Hashem*, "I love You." Like Moshe, who wrested the tablets of the ten commandments from *Hashem*, we can "fight" *Hashem* and win.

If we can use our free choice to go against *Hashem*'s will destructively — like Adam in the Garden of Eden, like the makers of the Golden Calf, like the murderers of Zechariah ben Yehoyoda — we certainly have the free choice to come back to *Hashem* despite all obstacles. After all, the bottom line is that *Hashem* wants us to win.

A Jew in Auschwitz could discover *Hashem*; he could — and many did — reaffirm his special relationship to *Hashem.* A survivor filled with doubt and bitterness can rediscover and announce his love of *Hashem.* And, in fact, I witnessed this.

Not long ago, a young woman — a European news correspondent — made a tour of America and came to one of my lectures. She liked the lecture, approached me afterwards, and told me her background. She was an assimilated Jew. Her father was a Holocaust survivor. Before the war he was Torah-observant, but then became very angry at *Hashem.* As a result, he had become vehemently anti-religious.

To make a long story short, the woman became fully Torah-observant in America and her father literally became sick over it.

He told her, "I ran as far away from religion as I could. And now you are coming back? Do you know what you are doing? Are you out of your mind!?"

I asked her to arrange a meeting between her father and me. She said, "He is so angry at you it is better that you do not meet him. He will not listen to anything." I had to back down and let the matter go.

Eventually, she decided to move to Israel. A while later, I came to Israel to give a series of lectures, one of which was in Tiberias. That woman was in Tiberias because her father had come to visit her and was staying at a local hotel. When she saw a poster announcing that I was lecturing, she came to see me.

I told her, "As long as your father is here, why not bring him to the lecture tonight?"

"No," she said, "he is still extremely angry at you."

"Nevertheless," I suggested, "why not recommend that he come to the lecture? What do you have to lose?"

"Okay. I'll try," she said.

That night, as I spoke, I did not know if they were in the audience or not. The lecture's theme was that the primary purpose of the Jewish people in this world is sanctification of *Hashem*.[82] My approach to that topic includes the various forms in which we can sanctify *Hashem*'s name. One way is through willingness to die for *Hashem*, another, and in many instances a more difficult way, is through willingness to live for *Hashem*.

To illustrate this concept, I told a story of Jews in Treblinka. Treblinka was one of the most brutal death camps; in less than a year some 800,000 Jews were slaughtered. And the Germans were not satisfied with merely killing Jewish bodies; as was said before, they wanted to denigrate the Jews and sully their souls.

The curtains which traditionally hung over the ark housing the Torah scrolls were hung over the entrance to the gas chambers. The wording on the curtains read: "This is the gate to *Hashem* the righteous walk through." The Nazis' intention was to cause the Jew to spend the last moment of his life cursing *Hashem*. The truth is it had just the opposite effect. When assimilated Jews saw this curtain inscribed with the words "the gate to *Hashem*," some of them woke up spiritually. They even danced and sang as they entered the chambers! They realized it truly was the gate to *Hashem* that they were entering.

This is what is called *kiddush Hashem* in death. However, there is another form of sanctifying *Hashem*'s name, I told the audience, which many times is much harder: it is *kiddush Hashem* in life; it is the *kiddush Hashem* of those who survived and rebuilt their lives. They saw the destruction and yet quietly went about the business of rebuilding their families, their communities, until they were ready to build a new synagogue and put up new curtains on which they wrote: "This is the gate to *Hashem* the righteous walk through." Their *kiddush Hashem* is perhaps an even greater sanctification of *Hashem*'s Name.

I concluded the lecture that night, "All of us here in this room are survivors of the Holocaust. Whether actual survivors of the Nazi concentration camps or survivors of the resultant spiritual Holocaust which rages on around us even now. Every Jew living today is a very real survivor of the Holocaust."

After the lecture ended, the woman walked over to me and said, "You know, my father was here tonight."

"Why not let us meet now?" I asked her.

She disappeared into the crowd and soon returned escorting her father. His head was bent forward. There was a long moment of pause. I did not know whether he was going to yell at me or break down crying. Finally, he said, "Rabbi, I want you to know that I was in Treblinka," he uttered with his voice cracking, "and I saw those very curtains that you spoke about tonight . . ."

He paused a few more moments, and then, his voice still choked with emotion, added, "I survived miraculously. And that is exactly why I became so angry. I was angry at *Hashem* for saving me. I asked myself a million times: Why did I survive? Why did I have to go through hell and then have to live with it? Is *Hashem* so cruel that He did not allow me to die with all my family and friends? Wouldn't that have been torture enough? Did He have to torture me with a living death?

"That is the pain I have been living with," he said. "That is why I became anti-religious. For all these years I could not answer that question: Why did I survive? Why did all those miracles happen to me which led to my survival? Was it just to cause me pain?"

I asked him, "Did you get your answer tonight?"

He nodded. He was choked up, though, and could not speak. I took the opportunity and said, "Although you thought that you could fight *Hashem* by building a secular family, nevertheless, your daughter found her way back. She is the one who is making those new curtains and inscribing on them: This is the gate to *Hashem*."

I looked at him and added, "When you see her living a meaningful Jewish life like your father's, isn't it clear to you how worthwhile it was to survive? You were not punished with life. You were rewarded with life, so your eyes could behold that."

He could not hold back any longer. He started crying

profusely. We made an appointment to meet shortly thereafter and eventually spoke for two hours. Afterward, his entire outlook and attitude were changed. He accepted his daughter like never before and was proud that she had found her way back to Torah.

Similarly, many, many — many! — of us are holding on to so much pain. However, no one is bereft of options when it comes to fulfilling the purpose we were created for: grasping for dear life onto Torah — the wedding ring, the unifier between *Hashem* and Israel. Both the Jew who survived the Holocaust and the Jew dying in the holocaust of a modern society which lacks moral boundaries and immune systems can discover the G-d of Israel and reclaim His Torah. The essential mission of a Jew — acknowledging and loving *Hashem* — is never withheld.[83]

The Pleasing Aroma

The calling card of the Jewish people is their willingness to sacrifice everything to complete the mission assigned to them by *Hashem*. This was Avraham. At a young age he smashed his father's idols. He suffered imprisonment and was thrown into a furnace for insisting that there was one G-d who had created the world with a specific purpose. Test after test, he reaffirmed his devotion to *Hashem*'s cause.

The trait of self-sacrifice is intrinsic to the Jew because of Avraham. In fact, it can be said that it even predates

Avraham's physical birth.

In a different post-Holocaust world — in the world of the earliest times — a man named Noah emerged from an ark. Surveying his new world, his emotions surged with a deep desire to express every tortured longing in his soul. He built an altar and performed sacrifices to *Hashem*. Concerning these sacrifices, the Torah says:

> And *Hashem* smelled the pleasing aroma. Then *Hashem* said to Himself, "No more will I destroy the earth because of man, for the inclination of the heart of man is evil from his youth. . ." (*Beraishis* 8:20,21)

What is the meaning of these words? Can *Hashem* be appeased by animal sacrifices? Was it really the smell of roasted meat which pleased *Hashem*? Of course not. It was the intention behind the sacrifice which pleased Him. What intention did *Hashem* "smell" in the actions of Noah? For a deeper understanding of this passage, we need to turn to *Chazal* of the *Midrash*. They write:[84]

> The pleasing aroma which *Hashem* smelled was the aroma of his [Noah's] descendant Avraham who would be willing to be thrown into the fiery furnace for *Hashem*'s sake.

Avraham was tested ten times. One of the tests occurred when he was thrown into a furnace (from which *Hashem* miraculously saved him) because he refused to renounce his belief in *Hashem*. That willingness to sacrifice his life for the truth is the "aroma" *Hashem* "smelled" in Noah's sacrifice. In other words, the act of sacrifice performed by Noah contained a foreshadowing of the self-sacrifice which would one day issue forth in all its fullness from Noah's descendant, Avraham.

The *Midrash* continues and tells us that the pleasing aroma contained even more intimations of future self-sacrifice. It also alluded to Chananiah, Mishael, and Azariah — the three Jewish youths who were thrown into the fiery furnace of King Nebuchadnezzar.[85] Like Avraham, they too were completely prepared to give up their lives rather than submit to a depraved ruler's request that they bow to an idol. And, like Avraham, *Hashem* miraculously saved them and let them walk out of the fire unscathed.

Finally, the *Midrash* adds, at the moment that Noah was performing his sacrifices, the pleasing aroma of yet another future act of Jewish self-sacrifice was detectable: the sacrifice of the generation of *shmad.*

Shmad means destruction through persecution, and can easily be translated as genocide or holocaust. One of the commentators on the *Midrash*[86] elaborates on the sacrifice of the generation of *shmad* as follows:

> Although Avraham as well as Chananiah, Mishael, and Azariah were miraculously saved from the fiery furnace, the generation of *shmad* will not. This generation will give up their lives sanctifying *Hashem*'s name, and actually have their bodies burned up [in the furnace].

This *Midrash,* then, sounds very much like it is referring to the generation of *shmad* which perished in the gas chambers and furnaces of the Nazi Holocaust. In fact, this contention is supported by an unbelievable recent find, a find made available with the advent of computer technology.

The Hidden Codes

By extending the principle idea contained in Rabbi Weissmandel's original discovery of the codes,[87] a computer was programmed to search the book of *Beraishis* to locate where the Hebrew equivalent of "Hitler" was spelled out in the smallest interval code. (The smallest interval means that even if the five letter name *heh-yud-tes-lamed-raish* [Hitler] was embedded in more than one place, the computer would identify the place where the smallest dispersion between these letters could be found. For example, if *heh-yud-tes-lamed-raish* was located in one place with 50 other letters between each of the five letters of Hitler's name, and in another place with only 20 letters between each of the letters, the 20 letter interval was assumed to be more significant.)

The computer searched and found that indeed Hitler's name was encoded in the Torah. The smallest interval code was 31,[88] found in our passage where *Hashem* smelled "the pleasing aroma" of the generation of *shmad* which would be completely consumed in the furnace!

Furthermore, the same verse uses the term *haAdam*

rah, "the evil man" when it states that "No more will I destroy the earth because *the* heart of *man [is] evil* from his youth." Who fits the description of "*the* evil man," if not Hitler?

Subsequent research revealed that not only was Hitler's name interwoven through this passage, but the highest concentration of lowest interval codes related to the Holocaust including the Hebrew equivalents of Berlin, Germany, Nazi, Auschwitz, gas chamber, Eichman, swastika (and others) were there as well!

This is not the place to elaborate on the specifics of this astounding find. At least as important as the discovery of the code itself is the message it supports, the message of the previously quoted *Midrash*: if any generation was the generation of *shmad*, it was the generation which perished in the gas chambers and furnaces of the Nazi Holocaust. (Although it is true that tragedies like the Crusades, the Spanish Inquisition, and the Cossack Massacres of 1648-1649 were carnages on a monstrous scale, the Holocaust contained the characteristics of an animal being led to slaughter. Jews were systematically transported, like animals, in cattle cars to an altar [i.e. a place designated specifically for their slaughter]. Never before in Jewish history had these elements of slaughter been present.)

The acts of Avraham, Chananiah, Mishael, and Azariah, as well as those of the generation of *shmad* are all linked in one 3,800-year-long chain. The Jewish nation began with Avraham. He was willing to give up his life in order not to desecrate the name of *Hashem* in the eyes of others. This essential trait in Avraham manifested generations later in Chananiah, Mishael, and Azariah. The timing of the latter three's sacrifice is significant. They lived at the beginning of the Babylonian exile, the first of the four exiles the Jewish people would have to endure. Their self-sacrifice and devotion served as a flag for Jews of all the ensuing exiles who would have to face life and death choices, and it sustained the Jewish people all the way until the generation of *shmad.*

The generation of *shmad* represents the final testing ground of the Jewish people's willingness for absolute self-sacrifice. They are the greatest testimony to Avraham's essential character since, as members of the last generations, they are the furthest removed from him and least likely to emulate him. Furthermore, they actually gave up their lives.

It is the generation of *shmad,* therefore, which puts the final stamp of recognition on the descendants of Avraham, Yitzchak, and Yaakov. It is such a holy generation that *Hashem* "smelled" its holiness at the time of Noah, and then declared: "No more will I destroy the earth because of man. . ." It was as if He was saying, "As long as I have such a self-sacrificing nation in My world, I will temporarily tolerate the cruelty of the non-Jews."

Every Slaughtered Jew A Martyr

While many Jews in the Holocaust, both simple and sophisticated, proved how devoted they were to *Hashem* — even under the most brutal circumstances — many did not. They did not understand what was happening to them. Some were even openly rebellious. How, then, can something like the Holocaust prove the love of the *kallah* Israel for the *Chasan* when many Jews did not sanctify *Hashem*'s name in their death?

In order begin to resolve this issue, it is important to note that Jewish history parallels the life of Avraham, the first Jew. Avraham's life foreshadowed what his descendants, the Jewish people, would have to endure. The *akeida,* the "binding" of Yitzchak — the tenth and final of Avraham's ten tests — parallels the ultimate challenge the Jewish people will have to face.

The key opening verses of the *akeida* read as follows:

> Avraham built an altar, laid out the wood, bound his son Yitzchak, and laid him on top of the altar, on top of the wood. Avraham stretched forth his hand and took the knife to slaughter his son. However, an angel of *Hashem* called to him from heaven and said: "Avraham! Avraham!"
>
> And he [Avraham] said, "Here I am."
>
> And he [the angel] said, "Do not stretch forth your hand [to slaughter] the boy; do not do anything to him. For now I know that you fear *Hashem*. . ." (*Beraishis* 22:9-12)

Upon scrutiny of the dialogue between Avraham and

the angel, a question arises: Why did the angel seem to repeat itself? If it said: "Do not stretch forth your hand [to slaughter] the boy. . . " why did it have to add: ". . . do not do anything to him"?

Chazal explain[89] that after the angel told Avraham to stop the first time, Avraham asked, "Let me at least make some small cut or mark on Yitzchak so that my coming here will not have been in vain." To this the angel responded, ". . . do not do anything to him." Thus, the angel's additional phrase was the response to Avraham's request to at least draw a little blood.

Now, only after this second remark by the angel did it declare: "Now I know that you [really] fear *Hashem.*" Why did the angel feel compelled to add that last remark? And what is the connection between Avraham's request to make a mark on Yitzchak and the acknowledgement that Avraham fears *Hashem*?

My brother, Reb Yechiel, *shlita,* the Rosh HaKolel of Mechon HaHoyroa, explains it as follows: According to Jewish law, one who is about to slaughter an animal is required to make a blessing before the slaughtering. Apparently, then, Avraham, no less than any ritual slaughterer, should have been required to say a blessing before performing the slaughter of his son. Therefore, when the Torah says, ". . . he stretched forth his hand to slaughter his son," self-apparent in that is that he had already said the blessing.

Then, all of a sudden, the angel said to Avraham,

"Stop! Do not stretch forth your hand. . ." What was Avraham's first reaction?

"What did I do?! A *bracha l'vatala*, a blessing in vain!" (In Jewish law, if one has actually said a blessing prior to some act, the act must be completed. Otherwise, it is a *bracha l'vatala*, a blessing said in vain, a matter not to be taken lightly.)

Avraham's entire being was attuned to performing *Hashem*'s will. By refraining from slaughtering Yitzchak after saying the blessing, he was in a quandary. He had said a blessing, but had not performed the act to go with it. That is why after the angel told him to stop, Avraham asked the angel if he could at least draw a little blood. Avraham wanted to at least perform a symbolic act to give fruition to the blessing he had said.

However, the angel told him to refrain even from that symbolic act of drawing blood. "Do not do anything to the boy" (i.e. do not even attempt to draw a little blood).

It was in this light that the angel proclaimed, "Now, I know that you fear *Hashem*. . ." as if to say, "Instead of rejoicing that the life of your son has been saved, the first thing on your mind is fulfillment of *Hashem*'s word. If you can show so much concern for performing *Hashem*'s will — worrying over saying a blessing in vain — when you are about to sacrifice your son, then you prove that you fear *Hashem*."

The Blessing in Vain?

To my brother's explanation I would like to add the following. Why didn't the angel allow Avraham to make a tiny mark? Why was it necessary to cause Avraham to make a *bracha l'vatala*? What happened to all that preparation Avraham had gone through before performing the most significant act of his life? Was it wasted? Was it literally in vain?

The *Gemara* says that *Hashem* attaches a good intention to a good deed.[90] In other words, if one has a good intention but circumstances do not allow him to fulfill his intention, *Hashem* takes that good intention and attaches it to another action. Indeed, we see many times that a person has a good intention but cannot bring it to fruition. Many other times, a person does something good but without the proper intentions. Thus, *Hashem*, in His mercy, takes the good intention and attaches it to the good deed.

For instance, one day a person prays with great feeling but nothing seems to happen. Another day, the same person is rushed and mouths his prayers perfunctorily, and the thing he prayed for the previous day comes about! What happened? *Hashem* took his good intention of the previous day and attached it to the second prayer.

(This occurs on the communal level as well. Some people want to do great acts of charity but have no money. Other people have a lot of money but donate it for their own fame or honor. All Jews are one, and therefore *Hashem* takes the intention of the pure-hearted Jew and attaches it to the money of the self-glorifying Jew, crediting the entire people with a single act of charity done with pure intentions.)

Over the centuries, and particularly during the Holocaust, Jewish people relived the traumatic dilemma of the binding of Yitzchak. Millions and millions of Jews, like Yitzchak, were brought to the slaughter. Occasionally, people knew what was about to happen to them and prepared themselves beforehand. However, many of these people had neither the opportunity nor the knowledge to recognize that they were giving up their lives for *Hashem*'s name. Some were just children. Others were unlearned. Still others had their minds go blank and their lips turn silent when they were torn from this world.

Nevertheless, they were all holy. It did not matter if the Jew did not understand or accept his end; *as long as he was killed because he was a Jew*, his death returned his soul to a state of purity and holiness. How could that be? What made that so?

The answer is Avraham's blessing-in-vain.

In truth, it was not in vain. Every thought, every preparation, every word of prayer and blessing that left his holy lips before he stretched forth his hand to sacrifice Yitzchak was attached to his descendants who did not have the opportunity to do so. Jews who died at the hands of Nazis, Europeans, Crusaders, Christians, Romans, and other bands of inhumane humans did not die a meaningless death — no matter how learned or unlearned, innocent or guilty they may have been. If they were slaughtered because they were Jews, their deaths made them holy.

Thus, when *Hashem* commanded Avraham to bring his son upon the altar as a sacrifice, Avraham actually fulfilled the command — however, there was a time lapse. Avraham made all the preparations with all the correct intentions. But it was not Yitzchak; rather it was for his future descendants who would fulfill the act intended for Yitzchak. They were the recipients of Avraham's preparations. His blessing was by no means in vain. The slaughter of Jews in all times is connected to the *akeida* — to the purity and holiness Avraham exhibited at the binding of Yitzchak.

Thus, the generation of *shmad* went into the furnace as a single chain extending back to Avraham. His intentions were attached to their actions and his merit ensured their immortality.

CHAPTER 6

THE AKEIDA

As discussed in the previous chapter, the *akeida* forms a direct link between Avraham and his descendants. As his life's greatest achievement, it brought to fruition a new and unique aspect of his personality that no other deed in his life accomplish. What did Avraham actually achieve with the *akeida*?

On the simplest level, it earned him a special blessing.

> [After the angel told Avraham that he knew he feared *Hashem*] Avraham looked up, and his eyes fell upon a ram caught in the thicket by its horns. Avraham took the ram and offered it up as a burnt offering in place of his son.
>
> The angel of *Hashem* called to Avraham a second time from heaven, saying, "By Myself, I make an oath, *Hashem* declares: because you have done this and not withheld

> your son, your favored one, I will bestow My blessing upon you and make your descendants as numerous as the stars of heaven and the sands of the seashore; and your descendants shall inherit the gates of their foes. All the nations of the earth shall be blessed through your descendants, because you obeyed My command. . ." (*Beraishis* 22:13-19)

In his comment on this verse, the Ramban explains that the blessing which *Hashem* gave Avraham guaranteed that his descendants, the Jewish people, would succeed with the mission for which they were chosen — no matter what obstacles would come their way. (This guarantee is described in the Torah as the "oath" *Hashem* swore to Avraham.)

This was no small matter. While it is true that *Hashem* promised Avraham earlier (67 years earlier at the "Covenant Between the Parts") that his children would become His representatives in this world, Avraham had not yet attained the merit sufficient to warrant this guarantee. Theoretically, at least, until the *akeida* his descendants could still have forfeited their destiny. However, after slaughtering the ram in his son's place, Avraham received the ultimate guarantee of his descendant's success. *Hashem* would in no way allow the Jewish people — *not even the least of them* — to abort their mission.

What exactly is their mission? What is a Jew's goal in life? And what exactly was it about the *akeida* which guaranteed Avraham that all his descendants, even the farthest removed, would fulfill their mission?

The answers to these questions will shed a brilliant new light on the theme of Jewish suffering. However, we need to start at the beginning.*

Yisroel, Torah, Creation

The process of creation took place in three stages. First came Yisroel (Israel). Yisroel is the "who" of creation: that entity which is the highest fulfillment of "the image of *Hashem.*" *Hashem* calls Yisroel: "My son, My first born."[91] The Maharal explains that the term "first born" in relation to *Hashem* means that the first existence outside of *Hashem* was Yisroel. Prior to performing any act of creation, *Hashem* detached a part of Himself, so to speak, and created Yisroel. In this sense, Yisroel preceded creation.

The second creation was Torah. It was created, to use the *Gemara's* terminology, "2,000 years before the creation of the world [but after Yisroel]."[92]

The third creation was the actual physical world.

These three — Yisroel, Torah, Creation — interrelate. Yisroel is first not only in a chronological sense, but in a conceptual sense as well. Yisroel is the focal point of creation. Fulfillment of its mission represents fulfillment

---

* Much of the following material can also be found in *Choose Life!* (especially Part I, Chapter 5, and Part II, Chapter 3) as well as in *To Become One* (Chapter 2).

of the purpose of creation. And that mission is to attain, through its own effort, reattachment to its Source, *Hashem.*

The vehicle by which Yisroel attains reattachment to *Hashem* is the physical world. Even though, by definition, matter is deficient in G-dliness, it is possible to infuse G-dliness into it. That is the primary mission of Yisroel. Yisroel's chore is to mix with the material in order to make positive use of this earthly existence so as to ultimately bring about an infusion of eternity into this otherwise temporal physical existence. By infusing transience with eternity, Yisroel's ultimate goal — reattachment with the Eternal One — is achieved.

What insures that a Yisroel will turn the physical into the spiritual, thereby making the reconnection to *Hashem*, rather than the other way around (that the material world will turn the spiritual Yisroel into a material creation, divorced from its Spiritual Source)?

Torah.

Torah is the connector. It teaches Yisroel how to interact with the physical world so that it is infused with spirituality.

Thus, Torah and Creation are the key elements Yisroel uses to fulfill the purpose of creation. Until Yisroel accomplishes this mission the world is an unfinished place. And that is our world: an unfinished place; it is still in the process of becoming complete, of attaining eternity.

Who Exactly is Yisroel?

Adam, the first man, was created at the apex of creation. The inanimate world, the vegetable world, and the animal world were his to "conquer" and use with the goal of infusing the physical with the spiritual. However, he was not created as Yisroel. He was only created with the chance to become Yisroel.

Adam had the choice to remain at the level at which he was created (i.e. a being with intelligence which placed him above the animal kingdom), or he could capitalize on his already high stature and raise himself even higher, to the level of a Yisroel. This choice manifested in the test of whether or not to listen to the Divine command forbidding him from eating of the tree of knowledge of good and evil.

As we know, Adam failed. Nevertheless, the potential which he lost remained available for any opportunistic and self-sacrificing person. Still, it took ten generations, from Adam to Noah, and ten more after Noah for an individual to pass all the tests necessary receive the status and soul of Yisroel.

Avraham was that individual. He was not happy being merely a human being. He realized that the real difference between a human being and an animal was not intellect. An animal, by definition, is restricted to following its instincts, whereas a human being can utilize free choice. True, a human being was also endowed with greater intelligence and more refined instincts than the animals, but what advantage was there to a human being's intelligence if he did nothing more than follow *his* instincts?

Thus reasoned Avraham. Therefore, he sought to utilize his free choice to elevate himself — to fulfill his maximum human potential. By doing so, he hoped to go beyond the status of a human being (whose potential for free choice is essentially unrealized) to the status of Yisroel (whose free choice is fully actualized).

Proper understanding of free choice is essential to this discussion. Before continuing with the accomplishments of Avraham, it is necessary to detour slightly and examine this concept of "free choice" in detail.

The Nature of Free Choice

If you naturally prefer sweet, and you have an opportunity to choose between sweet and sour, you really have no choice. You will choose only that which you naturally desire. The natural desire — by definition, something you were born with — is not something you toiled for, it is not something you chose to have. It was given to you at birth.

When can it be said that a person truly possesses free choice? When he possesses the ability to choose to go against his natural desires, his inborn preferences. Of course, some people have a tendency to go against their preferences merely for the sake of rebelling. However, that is rebellion for its own sake. That, too, is not really free choice; instead of being chained to an inborn physical preference, one is chained to his own psychological preference: the need to be different for its own sake.

Real choice is the ability to go against one's nature to make the correct choice because the choice is right, regardless of whether one's tendency toward that choice is inborn or bred, physical or psychological. It is just right, it is true.

How does one know what is right or true? The answer is simple: because *Hashem* says so, because the Creator prescribed it. Higher than human intellect, higher than human will, is the will of *Hashem*. It is the most significant factor in the universe. To truly fulfill one's potential as a human being, one has to go beyond his or her inborn human instincts to discern and then follow the will of *Hashem*.

People may object. "True freedom is the ability to choose to do what *I* want to do, not what anyone or anything else wants me to do — not even if that anyone or anything is *Hashem*!" At first glance, there is truth to that statement. By doing exclusively what *we* want, we are not obeying the wishes of another — *Hashem*; we are obeying our own wishes. One who follows such a path seems to be truly free.

Nevertheless, there is a flaw to such a line of reasoning. *Until we break down our inborn self, there is no self to talk about. Only when we rebuild our wants and desires independent of inborn preferences can we really exercise free choice. Otherwise, relying upon that inborn self in any way is just another form of enslavement: self-enslavement.*[93]

Thus, the only hope to escape the prison of self we are enclosed in from birth is to learn to forgo the *will of self* for the *will of Hashem*. That is called recreating one's self in the divine image. That process — and that alone — makes a human being more than an animal. In fact, it makes him more than a human being, because a human being is only an entity with the *potential* to utilize free will for the sake of obeying *Hashem*. However, one who truly *actualizes* his potential — who transcends inborn human will to serve the will of *Hashem* — is raised above the human race.

That is Yisroel.

Avraham: The Beginning

A Yisroel is not just anyone claiming to have transcended the inborn physical/animal side of his human nature. While it is easy for a person to intellectualize and say, "I give up my human will for *Hashem*'s will. I am now a Yisroel," it is another thing to actually do it.

To truly forgo one's will and align it with *Hashem*'s entails an act of submission so profound that it is, at its root, the most difficult conceivable task. To be totally committed to performing *Hashem*'s will while still vested in the garb of one's physical self — while still subject to the inclinations and passions of the body — is akin to actually putting one's very essence on an altar and slaughtering it. That is Yisroel.

And that was Avraham's goal.

Avraham wanted to be Yisroel — to permanently acquire the characteristics of Yisroel for himself and his descendants for all time. In order to do so, he had to first break down and then reconstruct his personal instincts so that his choices not be the result of certain in-born tendencies, but rather because he discerned *Hashem*'s will and became one with it.

Avraham not only had to overcome base instincts, such as the physical desires, but also the most essential and refined human instincts. For instance, he had to forgo his survival instinct and be willing to be thrown into a fiery furnace rather than submit to idol worship. He had to forgo his familial instincts when *Hashem* told him to abandon his father; separate from his nephew and disciple Lot; and banish his son Ishmael from his house. *Hashem* even told him to suppress his need to protect his beloved wife (when commanded to go to Egypt and forced to tell people that she was his sister for fear of his life.)

The tenth and final test, though, was his most challenging; it went right to the heart of his existence.

Avraham waited one hundred years for Yitzchak. One hundred years! And Yitzchak was not just a son to be proud of, someone to advance the good family name. Yitzchak was the culmination of everything Avraham had dedicated his entire life to. If he, Avraham, was to return the world to proper worship of the Creator, everything depended upon the unique, once-in-a-lifetime child worthy of the name Yisroel. Yitzchak was that child. And Avraham knew it.

Then *Hashem* said, "Take your son, your only son, the one whom you love — Yitzchak . . . and offer him up as a burnt offering. . ."

The test of the *akeida* went right to the core of Avraham's being. *Hashem* challenged Avraham to forgo the love of his son, the extension of himself — and in effect to forgo his love and hope for mankind. The continuation of Yisroel was the most noble goal possible and would eventually lead to the perfection of the entire world. However, now *Hashem* told him: Kill that possibility, kill your son.

To further illustrate the difficulty of the task, imagine *Hashem* told you to be a Hitler, G-d forbid, and slaughter all the Jews. What greater inhumane request could there be? Not only would that be genocide, but it would nullify the purpose of creation. Yet, that is exactly what *Hashem* commanded Avraham to do by slaughtering his "only son," Yitzchak.

Did Avraham ask questions? No. Did he even hesitate? No. In fact, "Avraham arose early [the next] morning [to fulfill *Hashem*'s will to bring Yitzchak as a sacrifice]." He completely nullified everything he knew to be true and holy. He nullified it because he knew that *there was nothing truer and holier than Hashem's word.*

To slaughter his son completely contradicted everything that *Hashem* represented (and everything Avraham had staked his reputation on when teaching the people of his time). Yet, he was one-hundred percent ready to do it because Avraham knew it was only his intellect which told him that slaughtering Yitzchak made no sense. And greater than his own intellect, his own life's philosophy — the philosophy which he knew to be true — was performing *Hashem*'s will.

The Essential Nature of the Sacrifice

In essence, *Hashem* was telling Avraham to slaughter more than his son Yitzchak. He was telling him to slaughter his own intellect.

To emphasize the magnitude of this sacrifice, we have to appreciate Avraham's intellect. First, do not harbor a common misconception that the ancients were not as smart as we are. The ancients possessed wisdom superior to ours in many ways. The principles of science and nature were open books to the ancients. They just did not have the technical apparatus we have today. In fact, around Avraham's time, the pyramids were being built. Today, with all our technology and science, we cannot rebuild the pyramids. Their construction continues to befuddle modern science.

If they were so smart, why did they worship idols? The answer is that their awareness of the machinations of nature — not their lack of awareness — led them along their path. They appreciated the value of the sun so much that they literally idolized it. They were so mind-boggled by the process of birth that they created gods and goddesses of fertility. Each component of the physical creation, with its impossible yet substantial beauty and perfection, so stunned them that they were blind to the interconnectedness of it all. They lost sight of the proverbial forest for the trees.

It is true that many simple people worshipped idols out of habit or to fulfill degenerate desires. Nevertheless, as the Rambam explains,[94] the original idol worshippers had the highest intentions. They were intellectually aware and sensitive people who became misguided. Their worship of many gods was originally based on an understanding of nature which we, of the technological age, take for granted.

Avraham was the greatest thinker of all time. He made a discovery greater than that of any contemporary scientist: there is one Creator. All the myriad components of the physical world are really one. When he looked at a tree, he saw how the fruits were good as a refreshing drink and as nourishing food. He saw how the branches were good for shade. He looked at a tree and said, "The Creator of this tree thought of everything — eating, drinking, lodging. A tree is a self-contained hotel.[95] Every part of it is perfectly designed for helping others. And each part is really the result of one coherent design produced by One Designer."

Thus, where others saw fruits, branches, and a trunk — and thought each component deserved worship as a separate god — Avraham saw the unity of the one benevolent Creator. As he advanced in years, his thinking advanced to the point where he was able to get to the root of every scientific fact available in his day, extract the kernel of truth from each, and find the common denominator. He did not just believe everything was connected. He could explain it — all of it.

Yet, *Hashem* said, "Slaughter your intellect; take everything you know to be true and noble, and sacrifice it on the altar. Show everyone that you know there is nothing higher than the will of *Hashem*. And since there is no intellect greater than yours, your sacrifice will be the ultimate sacrifice; it will constitute the highest price that can be paid."

Adam, in contrast, did not make the sacrifice. He, too, had profound intellect, perhaps even greater than Avraham's. The main difference was that while Avraham developed his mind over the years himself, Adam was created with perfect intellect. Adam did not have to develop his intuition and reasoning power himself.

The *Gemara* tells us Adam could see from one end of the world to the other.[96] In its deepest sense, that means he foresaw everything that would happen over history. Everything. He saw the downfall mankind and its ultimate elevation with the coming of *Moshiach*. We can even say that he knew that he would sin by eating from the tree of knowledge of good and evil. After all, if he could foresee everything, then he also foresaw that.

If so, one may ask, where was his free will?

He had the free will *not* to eat from the tree *despite* the foreknowledge that he would eat from it. In other words, his intellect told him, "I know that I am destined to eat from the tree of knowledge. This will result in the downfall of my descendants which will ultimately produce an incredible elevation in the days of *Moshiach.* In order to fulfill that destiny I must eat from the tree. Of course, *Hashem* has commanded me not to eat from the tree. However, I, with my intellect, know what is best. Furthermore, I know what the future holds: I am destined to eat from it. Therefore, I must disobey *Hashem*'s command and follow what I know to be true and good."

Avraham reasoned the exact reverse. "Even though I know that it is intellectually true that my son Yitzchak will be my successor and that slaughtering him undermines everything holy and good, nevertheless, what is my intellect — even my noblest and truest thought — in comparison to *Hashem*'s will? Therefore, I make the choice to forgo my intellect and follow *Hashem*'s command."

After Avraham did so, *Hashem* swore to him:

> "I will bestow My blessing upon you and make your descendants as numerous as the stars of heaven and the sands of the seashore; and your descendants shall inherit

> the gates of their foes. All the nations of the earth shall be blessed through your descendants, because you have obeyed My command. . ."

In other words, *Hashem* told him that he had permanently acquired the soul of Yisroel for himself and his descendants. He was the first to make the big breakthrough, to utilize free will in the ultimate way. He uncovered his Yisroel self hiding within his human soul.

Adam, in contrast, had the following exchange with *Hashem* after he misused his free will:

> And *Hashem* asked, "*Ayekah*, Where are you?"
>
> And he [Adam] replied, "I heard your voice in the garden and was afraid because I was naked; and I hid." (*Beraishis* 3:9,10)

Hashem of course knew where Adam was. His question to Adam meant to imply: Where is the true you, the Yisroel who chooses to forgo the will of mundane self for the will of *Hashem*?

To that, Adam replied, ". . . I was naked; and I hid." My "I" — my Yisroel self — the true self — was hidden. I was naked of it. Therefore, I was afraid to face You, knowing how I had failed to live up to its calling.

By contrast, when Avraham was told of his test of the *akeida,* his first reaction to *Hashem's* call was, "*Heenaynee*, Here *I* am." "I," my truest self — my Yisroel — am here. I, as a Yisroel, am ready to sacrifice that which is most holy and precious to me if You ask me to.

The result of Avraham's breakthrough in faith in *Hashem* was the permanent bestowal of the soul of Yisroel. Then he bequeathed everything to Yitzchak — and only Yitzchak[97] — who in turn gave the Avrahamic blessing to Yaakov,[98] upon whom the name, mission, and soul of Yisroel were officially and permanently conferred.[99] And every descendant of Yaakov is born part of this great collective soul called Yisroel. None of them can lose that aspect of soul, even if they want to.

A Jew has no In-between

Once Avraham permanently established Yisroel in this world, he traded in his status as a member of the human race and replaced it with an entirely new status: Yisroel. If so, one might think that a Yisroel who falls, falls to the level at which he began, that of a human being. However, this is not so. Once born a Yisroel, he can no longer be part of the human race. A Yisroel is either at the height of humanity, taking responsibility for it and raising it, or he is below humanity. There is no in-between. *A Yisroel who falls, falls below the level of a human being.*

This basic tenet is found in the *akeida*.

> And Avraham arose early in the morning and saddled his donkey. He took his two servants with him . . . On the third day, Abraham lifted his eyes and saw the place from

afar. Then Abraham said to his servants: "You stay here with the donkey. I and the boy [Yitzchak] will go up; we will bow down to G-d and then return to you. . ." (*Beraishis* 22:3-5)

The two servants were Ishmael, his son (through the concubine Hagar), and his devoted servant, Eliezer.[100] The *Gemara* says that when Avraham told Ishmael and Eliezer to stay with the donkey, he in effect told them, "Stay with the donkey, you [two] who are compared to a donkey."[101] Was Abraham intentionally trying to embarrass them? What did he mean by making the statement that they were donkeys?

The answer is that despite his best efforts to improve Ishmael and Eliezer, there was a point they could not go beyond. That point came when he said, "You [two] stay here with the donkey," with your physicality (donkey, *chamor* in Hebrew, also translates as "physicality"). Meanwhile, "The boy [Yitzchak] and I will go up. . ." Yitzchak and I will ascend to become truly spiritual, to become Yisroel.

He was not insulting them by comparing them to the donkey. He was simply indicating that the demarkation between he and Yitzchak and them was the willingness to perform the *akeida* — to forgo human will to the extent that one is even ready to sacrifice that which is most dear to oneself. And that is what he and Yitzchak did. They left their physical nature completely and totally behind by showing their willingness to follow G-d despite the apparent consequences.

At the *akeida,* Avraham's descendants lost the ability to ever truly consider themselves an equal with the human race. They would have to live up to the calling of Yisroel or fall below the human race. This thought is also present in the oath *Hashem* "swore" to Avraham at the *akeida*: "I will multiply your offspring as the stars of heaven and the sand upon the seashore." Jews can either be the stars of heaven which radiate light upon the earth, or they are the sand on the seashore everyone tramples upon. They are at the top or at the bottom. They are no longer like everyone else.

We even find this tenet in the very names by which the third Patriarch is known: Yaakov and Yisroel. Yaakov's name comes from the verse: *yaudo ochezes b'akev Esav*, "his hand is holding the heel of Esav."[102] The heel is the lowest part of the body. Thus, naming Yaakov for the act of lunging for the heel of his brother at birth teaches that the name Yaakov indicates pursuit of the lowest material urges. On the other hand, the Zohar tells us that the letters of the name Yisroel spell *li rosh*, "to Me is the head." Thus, the Jew is either Yaakov, having to satisfy himself with the lowest part of his materialistically inclined brother Esav, or he is Yisroel, at the top.

The idea that a Jew cannot be "in-between" — that he has to be spiritually at the top or at the bottom — is a sensitive point and warrants clarity. Let us explain it further by analyzing the words of Shlomo HaMelech.

The Tzevaos and the Rams of the Forest

"I [*Hashem*] swear by you, the daughters of Jerusalem, [regarding] the *tzevaos,* soldiers [of *Hashem*] and the rams of the forest: Do not shake up the love which I have for them; and do not stir up the love they have for Me, *ahd sh'techpatz*, until I will send you to do it." (*Shir HaShirim* 2:7)

Rabbi Yaakov Lissa[103] explains that the "daughters of Jerusalem" refers to the nations of the world, the non-Jews, while both the *tzevaos* [of *Hashem*] and "the rams of the forest" refer to Jews.

Tzevaos means soldier in the sense of a representative of the ruler or nation who sent him to fight. The Jewish people, the *tzevaos* of *Hashem*, are the soldiers — the representatives — of *Hashem* in this world. They are faithful to the directives (i.e. Torah) of the One who sent them into this world.

Nevertheless, some Jews (out of ignorance, arrogance, or some other reason) are not devoted to the directives of the One whom they represent. Although their souls are very much the souls of Yisroel, the way they live their lives are not truly representative of Yisroel. They are more aptly described as the wild rams of the forest, who do not particularly represent anyone. They are Yisroels whose potential remains essentially unfulfilled.

Now, concerning these two groups of Jews, *tzevaos* and rams, *Hashem* sends a directive prophetically conveyed by Shlomo HaMelech. To the "daughters of Jerusalem," the non-Jews, *Hashem* says: do not "shake up" the *tzevaos* and do not "stir up" (arouse) the rams of the forest. If the Jew is a *tzevaos,* do not "shake up" the good relationship I, *Hashem*, have with him. If, on the other hand, he is like a ram of the forest, do not "stir him up" — do not stir or influence him toward *teshuva,* returning to *Hashem*, repentance.

Why would *Hashem* not want the Jewish "rams-of-the-forest" to do *teshuva*? The answer is: in reality, He does. He wants them to do *teshuva* more than anything else, in fact. However, He does not want the non-Jews to be the ones to initiate that *teshuva*; He wants to give all Jews the great opportunity to "return" of their own volition. Thus, *Hashem* tells the non-Jew not to stir up the Jew — at least not until *ahd sh'techpatz*, "until I will send you to do it." How can the non-Jew stir up and arouse the non-Torah Jew to *teshuva,* to a return to *Hashem*? Paradoxically, the answer is anti-semitism.

We know that many Jews returned, in their hearts at least, to identification with Jews and Judaism when the German and other European peoples bared their fangs. That is the paradox of anti-semitism. Historically, it has always stimulated camaraderie and sentiment for Judaism among Jews otherwise unstimulated.

Hashem tells the non-Jews not to try to effect the Jew, whether he be *tzevaos* or the ram, *ahd sh'techpatz*, "until [the time comes when] I will send you to do it." The emphasis is on *I* — until *I* want this to happen. That will be the last generation before *Moshiach,* when *Hashem* can no longer wait for them. Then He will send the daughters of Jerusalem, the non-Jews, to do it.

As the *Gemara* explains, at that time "I will send you a ruler as harsh as Haman."[104] He will take both types of Jews and carry out a holocaust. The Jew who is *tzevaos* will be tested: Are you really a *tzevaos*, or will this "shake up" your faith in Me? If you remain firm, you have really proven yourself.

As for the Jew who is far from his spiritual roots, the non-Jew will hunt him like a ram. As hunters take pride in the number of wild animals they have "bagged," so will the Nazi take pride in the number of Jews he will have exterminated. However, this virulent anti-semitism will serve as a stimulant to otherwise spiritually numb Jews and help them return to *Hashem,* as we have just explained.

Connection to the Akeida

The words in *Shir HaShirim* echo the event which took place at the very inception of Yisroel's history, the *akeida*. Notice that the *akeida* really has two parts. The first part is Avraham's sacrifice of Yitzchak, which was prevented at the last second by an angel from heaven. The second part is Avraham's sacrifice of the ram caught in the thicket (which Avraham sacrificed literally as if it were his son). The Torah itself draws this distinction regarding the two parts of the *akeida* when it says that the angel called "a *second* time." This second call occurred immediately after Avraham sacrificed the ram, and signals a second part to the *akeida*.

Thus, there are two types of Jews: *tzevaos* and the rams of the forest. Each corresponds to one part of the *akeida*. Yitzchak is the equivalent of the *tzevaos* Jew mentioned in the verse of *Shir HaShirim*, the Jew whose lifestyle is representative of *Hashem*'s will. And the ram that Avraham sacrificed is, then, obviously the ram mentioned in the verse in *Shir HaShirim*. And the fate of these two Jews is described in the two parts of the *akeida*.

If a Jew is like Yitzchak, a Yisroel who willingly sacrifices everything, there is no need to go through with the actual sacrifice. This Yitzchak-*tzevaos*-type Jew's very life is the epitome of self-sacrifice, and as in the first part of the *akeida*, the angel calls from heaven at the last moment to rescue him.

However, if the Jew is more like the wild ram of the forest, there is a dilemma. Avraham won a guarantee from *Hashem* that all his descendants would be Yisroel. However, this Jew is not summoning up within himself the necessary self-sacrifice, the subjugation to *Hashem*'s will, that characterizes Yisroel. The solution to this dilemma is that the sacrifice has to be initiated by an outside source. *Hashem* has to restore his status as Yisroel through an actual sacrifice.

Avraham irrevocably infused this deep historical structure into the life pattern of his future descendants with the second part of the *akeida,* the sacrifice of the ram in place of Yitzchak. If a Yisroel does not voluntarily exploit the opportunity to sacrifice his everything on the altar of *Hashem*, then his "everything" gets sacrificed, like an animal, on the altar by others. A Yisroel, a descendant of Avraham, is designated for a unique purpose. He is either a Yitzchak or a ram for slaughter. It is an all-or-nothing situation. There is no in-between.

Avraham set up this all-or-nothing situation to benefit his descendants. As said above, our goal in life is to recreate ourselves in the image of *Hashem* by using free will to exchange the will of self for the will of *Hashem* — to exchange the mundane for the holy. This produces a transcendance of self that is ultimately the most pleasurable experience imaginable. It is a tremendous challenge to realign our will to *Hashem's* will, though, because from birth our initial identification is with the mundane aspects of our self and thus our tendency is to not always follow our G-dly instinct. Nevertheless, the sacrifice of the physical is ultimately the healthiest food for the soul. It allows our natural holiness to burst forth and it is that experience which is the most wonderfully rewarding.

Torah — *Hashem's* will, His "instructions" — is designed to keep a Jew focused on the life of the spirit even as he is engaged in the physical. While demanding that he eat, marry, interact with others and generally take part in a physical life, the 613 commandments force the Jew, every single day, to make choices between the material and the spiritual — every single day. For instance, we wish to eat whatever we want, but the Torah tells us to only eat *kosher.* We want to hoard money and possessions, but the Torah commands us to give and give and give. Fifty . . . one hundred . . . two hundred times every day, we are asked to give up a part of our stake in the material world.

Both the Yitzchak-*tzevaos*-type Jew and the ram-type Jew are holy. Both are the embodiment of Yisroel. The Torah-cognizant Jew is holy through his own actions during life, through his daily, constant effort to transcend the mundane. The Jew who was inattentive to or negligent of Torah does not possess sufficient holiness to help him transcend the mundane. However, his right as a descendant of Avraham guarantees that he is destined for ultimate holiness and transcedance of self. Thus, if he never attains holiness through his life, the *akeida* guarantees that he will attain it through his death.

This is what Avraham accomplished with the *akeida.* By sacrificing the ram in place of Yitzchak, Avraham was insuring that even his future descendants who would abandon their association with Avraham and the mission of Yisroel — and who by so doing would drop down to the level of a ram of the forest — even they would ultimately earn the stature for which they were created — to be infused with holiness.

This message is further implied in the oath *Hashem* swore to Avraham that his descendants would be like the stars of heaven and the sand upon the seashore. If they were worthy like the stars of heaven — the *tzevaos* — they would attain greatness, holiness, and immortality just as the stars symbolize those qualities. And even if they would be trampled as the sand on the seashore — the ram led to slaughter — they would be indestructible just as the sand is enduring. Even a Yisroel who does not live up to his potential in life is guaranteed his gift of an immortal soul.

It is important to emphasize is that it is never too late. A Jew who has abandoned the Torah can always reclaim his status as Yisroel during his lifetime. And that option remains open to him until the moment he dies, no matter how far away he is from Torah. Even for a Yisroel who is so far gone that a meaningful return to Torah is highly improbable, there is a solution. The Nazis called it the Final Solution. It is shocking and something we do not like to think about, let alone admit, however, Jewish history speaks for itself.

Who understands the purpose for which we were put in this world? Of those who truly attained this level of understanding, no one understood that purpose as acutely as Avraham. Yet, he chose this all-or-nothing fate for his descendants. We, in our often myopic view of life, do not genuinely appreciate what we have in our hands. Life is not a picnic. It is an opportunity to create our selves — to create our selves by nullifying our will and rewiring it to align with *Hashem*'s will. If we do not pursue that with every fiber of our being and during every moment we breathe, then we are not really living.

Life is the opportunity to earn for ourselves the identity of Yisroel. And if one is not able to do that in life, he should at least be able to do it in death. That is the significance of the blessing — the guarantee — to Avraham that his descendants would never fail. They would forevermore be Yisroel whether through self-motivated fulfillment of their potential — through their self-sacrifice — or through their sacrifice by others.

Civilization and the Germans

This all-or-nothing situation is bound to disturb some readers. A Yisroel living a life devoid of Torah cannot say, "Oh well, nothing lost, nothing gained. I was born a Yisroel, but I prefer to live my life free of the responsibility of following *Hashem*'s will as laid forth in the Torah. I am happy to just be a good human being." A Yisroel does not have the option to count himself as an equal among the human race. He is either a Yitzchak raising himself to the heavens, or a ram of the forest ripe for the slaughter.

If this sounds shocking to you, you are not alone. It would have sounded especially shocking to the German Jew in pre-Hitler Germany. After all, German culture was the height of humanity. For over a century, German

Jews had assimilated into German culture to the point they could honestly say they had no relationship to their outdated religion. They had come of age, they had "caught up." They were part of humanity now.

Hitler changed that. He claimed that they were below humanity, that they had no share in it, and certainly no share in the peak of humanity he called German culture. And a staggering majority of the "civilized" world believed him, or at least remained silent about his claims.

Hitler hated Jews because they were different, even though they were trying their hardest to prove to the world that they were not. In so doing, he detected an essential factor, which Jews themselves had failed to recognize and acknowledge: a Jew is not to be counted among humanity. He is either above it, taking responsibility for it, or he is below it, classified by others as a subhuman.

When the Jew tries to take part in humanity as the non-Jew, the non-Jew looks at him and thinks (consciously or subconsciously): "This is one of the chosen people? He does nothing more than I do. He wants nothing more than I want. I resent him for not being himself, for not being more than me. I resent him for not raising me, for not helping me set my sights higher. All he wants is to be like me."

Of course, the non-Jew did not always express this sensitivity to the difference between himself and the Jew in the form of mere resentment. Sometimes it was seething jealousy. "By trying to assimilate with me, he is taking away that which belongs to me. He is taking away my job, my house, my wife, my patriotism, my idealism, my lifestyle." (As the saying goes, he is trying to "out-German the Germans.")

As the assimilation continued, the jealousy burned. It burned and certain elements of the populace expressed their feelings . . . loudly. The more civilized elements — the polite ones — felt the same way but did not express it as openly. They became the obedient masses in Nazi-infested Europe who claimed not to see the deportations and round-ups, who afterwards maintained that they did not smell the burning flesh emanating from the smoke-stacks of the nearby concentration camp. They were the "good human beings" who turned their eyes and pretended that they just did not see.

When a Jew tries to be an equal to the human race, he is eventually reminded that he is not. The more he tries to become part of humanity, the more humanity is repelled and pushes him down. It may not happen immediately, but a Jew who drops from his stature as Yisroel will eventually be viewed as a subhuman; and not long thereafter, may find himself as an animal led to the slaughter.

The Ram Caught in the Thickets

The parallels between the *akeida* and the Holocaust do not stop here. Indeed, they run very deeply, and the symbolism is very significant.

> On the third day, Avraham lifted his eyes and saw the place from a distance . . . (*Beraishis* 22:4)

According to the Chasam Sofer, the phrase "on the *third* day" is actually an allusion to the fact that Avraham saw the time and place of the Third *Bais HaMikdash*. Although the era of the Third *Bais HaMikdash* epitomizes universal peace and spiritual growth, the events that lead into it are described as birthpangs (i.e. times of upheaval). It is that time of upheaval, the Chasam Sofer remarks, that Avraham saw when he "lifted his [spiritual] eyes" toward the future and perceived it.

This wording, "he lifted his eyes," is repeated just nine verses later:

> And Avraham *lifted his eyes* and he saw a ram caught in the thickets by its horns. (*Beraishis* 22:13)

Applying the Chasam Sofer's explanation of verse 4, verse 13 means to say that Avraham "lifted his [spiritual] eyes" and saw into the future again. What did he see? The ram. Who is the ram? The future generation of his descendants who would lose their identity as Yisroel and appear as a ram for the slaughter. Who is that future generation? My contention is that the Holocaust was the true fulfillment of the *akeida*.

Until the Holocaust, never in history had there been a

civilization which took human fat and used it to make soap, or which used human skin to make lampshades, or which slaughtered people and used their hair to make wigs, or which ran medical experiments on people like on guinea pigs. And not only that, but all the above was accomplished by first squeezing Jews into *cattle* cars so that they could be systematically rounded up into a central place for their slaughter. Jews were treated as animals. Literally.

The Holocaust was the *akeida* fulfilled. The gas chambers of Nazi Germany served as Avraham's altar. It was there that the Jew was sacrificed on the altar as if he were an animal.

Avraham looked into the future and saw a "ram caught in the thicket by its horns." As we said, the ram is Avraham's descendants, the Jews who will lose their identity as Yisroel (*tzevaos*) and instead appear as rams of the forest. Of course, that Jew will not view his own actions as something which lowers him to the level of an animal. That Jew will first descend from his stature as Yisroel and consider himself an equal of all other humans. However, humanity will not accept him. Instead, humanity will treat him as an animal, a ram.

The ram Avraham sees is tangled in the thickets. This means that the Jew will be entangled in something that will make him an easy prey for the slaughter; that "something" is the non-Jewish culture, humanity. And the ram will become entangled by its horns. The horns of a ram are the very things which symbolize the animal, its pride. The Jew who assimilated and out-Germaned the Germans saw his solidarity with the cause — with the fatherland — as a source of pride and achievement. However, it was the very thing in which he became entangled, and was ultimately his undoing.

Imagine if the original German Jew who came to so idolize German culture could have been alive a century later, in 1940. What would he have thought of his decision to abandon Torah for German-European-Christian humanity and culture? Of course, he may not have admitted to the association between his abandonment of Torah ideals and the rise of Naziism. He idealized the beauty of German culture and philosophy. He was so blindly in love with it, in fact, that he probably was incapable of following it to its logical conclusion.

However, Hitler and the Nazis did follow through. The Fuhrer listened passionately to his favorite composer, Wagner (himself an open anti-semite), whose haunting operas glorified Germany's past and fermented the longing for a racially pure German people who would one day live triumphantly and domineeringly in the beloved fatherland. While Germany's original assimilated Jews closed their ears to the implications of Wagner's tones, the Nazi forefathers heard in the resonating compositions the "sieg heil" of the multitudes with stretched forth arms, and palms straightened in homage to the leader of the German master race.

Of course, the German culture which nineteenth century Jews so idolized was not limited to just Wagner and music. In the profound philosophy and poetry of Nietzche, to mention just one example, the same Nazis read of the "superman," and extended the idea to create the underpinnings of a philosophy which saw Germany as the master race.

German-Christian religion, too, earned the envy of the German Jew. Reform Judaism, now not even two centuries old, began in Germany less than a century before the rise of the Nazis. A handful of Jewish individuals declared their belief that the Torah as practiced for centuries and centuries was no longer binding. They were unabashed in their preference for the outer trappings of German-Christian culture, so (among other things) they exchanged Hebrew for German in their prayerbooks, Jerusalem for Berlin as the capital of their promised land, and the teachings of Moses for those of Moses Mendelssohn (most of whose grandchildren voluntarily converted to Christianity).

Strangely, the Reformers did not claim to deny the Torah. They claimed to only be "re-forming" it. However, in reality, they were "conforming" it (or "deforming it") to align with their own understanding, which drew heavily, if not primarily, on the cultural understanding of the times.

But times and cultures change. What was considered "universal" in one place at one time is no longer universal in another place at another time. European-style nationalism and pride in the fatherland were in vogue when the early Reformers sought to "re-form" the Torah to their understanding. Thus, they fired up their followers with speeches denigrating the clinging to outdated religious practices which seemed only to isolate Jews from their German brethren. "Be a Jew in the home but a German in the street" went the motto. In the nineteenth century German synagogue it was perfectly normal, and in fact progressive to laud the German fatherland. One who denied the utopian vision and destiny of the German nation was accused of living behind the times.

The early Reformers led their flock and became more and more German, to the point where their synagogue was more church than synagogue. Their rabbis dressed like Christian clergy, their services became characterized by organ music, their prayerbooks became German, and their longings for Berlin. And, above all, they were convinced that the ethical standard of German culture was by far an improvement over the crude, outdated religion of the Torah.

Music, poetry, philosophy, religion — in the irony of history the German Jew and the Nazi both idolized the same gods. The German Jew deluded himself, though, and could not see how his prostration before the Baal of modern, "enlightened" Europe was no less a path to self-destruction than was fidelity to blatant, cruel paganism.

Even foreknowledge of the logical extension of nineteenth century German culture probably would not have detoured the assimilated German Jew from his chosen path. He loved his German music, his German poetry, his German nationalistic pride, his symbiotic identity with German religion and culture. He thought of it as his own. Had he known what it would amount to a century later, he probably would not have been able to disentangle himself from it. German culture was the horn of his pride. And by it, he was ensnared. He was the ram Avraham saw caught in the thickets.

This is the inevitable outcome of a Jew who discards his identity as Yisroel. The German Jew did everything to assimilate and repudiate his status as Yisroel. Hitler and the German people, however, did not accept the Jew. Instead, they created the Nuremberg Laws in 1935, effectively isolating the Jew within German society in the exact way the Torah had specified to the Jew. Whereas the exhortations of *Hashem*'s prophets were not enough to curb Jewish assimilation and intermarriage, the Nuremberg Laws effectively stripped the Jew of his German citizenship and prevented marriage or any type of relationship with Aryans. Whereas the words of the sages to discourage Jews from attending the theaters and stadiums of the non-Jews proved futile in Germany, the Nuremberg Laws decreed that Jews were forbidden to congregate anywhere except the synagogue. Whereas the Torah's command for Jews to dress differently from gentiles was abandoned, the Nuremberg Laws forced Jews to wear a yellow star of David on their clothing.

Thus, the Nuremberg Laws isolated the Jew within German society in the exact way the Torah demanded. The tragedy was that the Nuremberg Laws were imposed from without, and once more drove home the sad but true lesson of Jewish history: if the Jew does not voluntarily follow the Torah laws, then outsiders, in an unfriendly way, impose them.

The Nazis unwittingly achieved the exact opposite of what they hoped to achieve. They detected the essential quality of a Jew that Jews themselves denied. While Jews were trying their hardest to prove to the gentile world that they were the same, the Nazis acknowledged that Jews were different. No Jews epitomized this more than the German Jews. They were the first to openly break with Torah tradition, to denigrate it, and proudly devote their lives to advancement of the non-Jewish society about them. Then the German people came and showed them that they were foreigners, non-Aryans, subhumans. The fact that Jews were treated as animals proved that they had no place in humanity. And the Nazis proved that point better than anyone before.

The message for the Jew was and is: you are not an equal partner in humanity; you have a higher calling — the highest calling. You are Yisroel! Invest at least as much in that calling as you did in the culture of Germany, of "humanity." Sanctify your life with Torah in order to avoid the necessity of becoming sanctified through death.

The Shocking Truth

If all this is shocking . . . then, yes, it is shocking. A shock is something meant to awaken a sleeping person — and not just a sleeping person, but a person in a deep sleep, perhaps even in a coma. A Yisroel either recognizes his higher calling or he is reminded, pinched, and ultimately shocked into realizing that wishy-washiness or hiding safely-in-between as a "good human being" is not an option. It is all or nothing. And it is part of *Hashem*'s mercy that He set it up that way, for otherwise the Yisroel would not achieve the purpose for which he was created.

There is no advantage in Yisroel denying his or her identity and settling on some other sense of self. The truer one is to oneself, the greater the benefit in the long run — despite what it may seem in the short run. The ultimate good a person untrue to himself can experience is the destruction of that inflated or symbolic self.

Think of money. Originally, the monetary system was backed with real value. There was a dollar. Every dollar stood for gold or silver locked away in a safe. Furthermore, a half-dollar, a quarter, a dime were made of silver equal to their value. The actual value — the silver — and the symbolic value — the purchasing power of the coin — were one and the same. When the cost of silver went up, the purchasing power went up. When the cost of silver went down, the purchasing power went down.

That was in the old days.

Then, inflation set in. Purchasing power became independent of metal value, and more and more associated with symbolic value. Soon, people began to realize that the symbolic value was seriously out of proportion to its actual backing. When that happened the metal coin itself became five to ten times more valuable than the purchasing power of its symbolic value. The silver quarter was worth two dollars on the silver market.

As a result, some people stopped trading currency and instead began collecting coins and melting them into solid bars to be sold at market value. (That is why you no longer find real silver currency.) It did not matter what the symbolic value had been. Melted half-dollars, quarters, and dimes all became part of the same bar of silver.

Usually, the symbolic value enhances the actual value. However, when the symbolic value becomes so inflated that it is almost an entity unto itself, the destruction of the symbolic value leads to the restoration of the actual value. The general rule is: *whenever the symbolic value becomes inflated and unreal, only the real value counts, and, in fact, becomes more valuable and desirable.*

The same analogy applies to the Yisroel. There is the actual value, the essence of a Jew. A Jew is that species of human being whom *Hashem* chose for a special mission on this earth.[105] And there is the symbolic value of the Jew, the expression of his Jewishness. The Jew expresses and manifests his election by *Hashem* through imbuing himself with Torah practice and teachings — the symbolic value.

When the Jewish people were healthy, every symbolic value had its backing. The rabbi was an authentic rabbi; he was valued for his Torah knowledge. The leader was valued for leadership. Every position, every ritual — every expression of symbol — had its coverage. And that is the ideal: when the symbol is a true expression of the essential.

However, the situation deteriorated from the inside. Despite the outer trappings, a very significant percentage of Jews in pre-Hitler Europe were leaning toward or already floundering in assimilation, communism, and many other "isms." The religious strongholds, too, were showing cracks. Far too many Jews had never learned, forgotten, or harbored misgivings about on their real identity, their real sense of self-worth.

Then Hitler arose. He was the Jew detector. Just as a metal detector detects metal, he detected Jews. If they were intermarried for five generations (and he did not stop with mere matrilineal descent), Hitler found them in their pews at Church on Sunday morning. He found them wearing the medals they won fighting for Germany in World War I. He found them all — wherever they were, whatever their status. Jews who had separated from each other because they had clung to their symbolic value were collected and stripped of their superficial, inflated differences.

There is a story of a seventy-year-old assimilated German Jew deported to a camp in the final days of World War II. All day he would cry out, "It's all my fault. It's all my fault."

When people would ask him what he meant, he would remain silent, too embarrassed to speak. Finally, one concentration camp inmate convinced him to reveal his story.

"It's my fault," he said. "I did not listen to my mother fifty years ago. Fifty years ago, my mother begged me not to marry a gentile. I thought, 'What does my mother, this old woman know?' I did not listen to her and married the German woman anyway. We had a wonderful relationship and built a beautiful family. I have many children and grandchildren. One day, this beautiful family of mine came to me and told me, 'Father, you are a Jew. You don't belong with us. Why don't you go with all the other Jews?' And then they reported me to the gestapo. My own children! My own wife! It's all my fault! It's all my fault! My old-fashioned mother knew more than me! I should have listened to her."

Hitler did not care about the externals, the symbolic value. He took the westernized sophisticated Jew and the Polish peasant Jew and threw them both into the same camp, the same melting pot. All were melted into the same bar of soap.

Stripped of the artificial, the Jew was confronted with his real value. In this way, Hitler made *kodoshim* of the rams-of-the-forest Jews regardless of what they were before. He caused them to rediscover their true self-worth. (See Question 7 in the Appendix for more.)

We are obligated to find out who we are while we are alive. When we do, we develop real value; we give backing to our symbolic value. If we discover our own value, our own identity, by ourselves, then *Hashem* does not need to send a crazed gentile Jew detector.

More than nuclear physicists, doctors, international bankers, politicians, psychologists, and the like, the world needs healthy, responsible Torah-observing Yisroels. Better than Jews killing themselves to fulfill the American dream are Jews willing to live an American nightmare (of financial mediocrity), if it so has to be, in order to achieve Torah ideals. The more a Jew realizes and appreciates what it means to be a Yisroel, the better he is and the better the world is. If Yisroel ceases to exist, or he exists in a collective spiritual coma, a vacuum of global proportions exists — a vacuum in which Hitlers, Nazis, Hamans, and Amaleks germinate.

We Jews cannot escape our destiny. Either we struggle with the difficulty of living up to being Yisroel or face the inevitable sadistic wake-up call from a never-ending supply of anti-semites. We have to become who we are or face the fact that others will identify us in ways which may shock us. *Hashem* set it up that way to benefit us — so that, one way or another, we would have no choice but to fulfill our real destiny.

The Ohr Chodosh

An obvious question remains. In the *akeida, Hashem* dispatched an angel to halt the slaughter of Yitzchak at the last moment. In Nazi-Europe, however, no angel called from heaven at the last moment to stop the slaughter. While it is true that the deterioration of Jewish life was occurring at an ever-increasing rate, even in the religious strongholds, many *tzevaos* Jews were slaughtered by the Nazis. If they were truly righteous Jews, in every sense of the term, why were they slaughtered?

This question can be answered, however, perhaps it is presumptuous to do so, since the suffering of the righteous is an age-old question that even the likes of Moshe and Iyov (Job) struggled with. (See Question 7 in the Appendix for an answer to this question.) Rather than asking "Why were they slaughtered?" a better question would be "What was gained by their slaughter?" or "What did they think was gained by their slaughter?"

Rabbi Elchonon Wasserman *zt'l*, considered the greatest disciple of the holy Chofetz Chaim, was head of the Branovich Yeshiva. He traveled to America in 1939 to collect funds. When the war broke out, he decided to return to Europe and share the fate of his brethren.

Despite attempts to dissuade him, he would not abandon his community although he was well aware of the dire events about the befall European Jewry.

When the Branovich yeshiva was relocated by the Nazis to the Kovno Ghetto, he continued teaching and leading others. Finally, the day arrived when the Nazis were to exterminate them. Rabbi Wasserman's final lecture, recorded by a disciple who survived, covered the topic of *kiddush Hashem.*

"It seems," he said in his powerful, noble yet humble voice, "that in heaven they consider us righteous, because they have chosen us to atone with our bodies for all Jews. Time is short. We have to know that when they slaughter us, the better and purer our intentions the greater the merit we will earn to save our brothers and sisters in America. Bad thoughts that arise in our minds now are like *pigul.* (According to Torah law, a *pigul,* an impurity, invalidates the sacrifice one brings to be slaughtered on the Temple altar.) You have to be aware that we are now fulfilling one of the greatest *mitzvos, kiddush Hashem.* We say in our prayers, "In fire You destroyed the *Bais HaMikdash*, and in fire You will rebuild the *Bais HaMikdash.*" That same fire which will burn up our bodies, will be the fire which will rebuild a new Jewish nation."

Since Rabbi Wasserman was in America before the war broke out, he saw the terrible deterioration of the Jewish community there and was concerned over their spiritual welfare. He was convinced that his slaughter, and the slaughter of those *tzevaos* Jews like him, would atone for the Jews of America, earning them the merit necessary to rebuild spiritually. It is not coincidence, in my mind, that the Teshuva Movement really started in America, and only then spread to Israel from where it spread throughout the Jewish world. The pure, final thoughts of righteous people, like Rabbi Wasserman and his students, who gave their life up in the fires of the Holocaust, form the foundation of merit upon which the Jewish world is currently building anew.

Only *Hashem* knows exactly why He did not dispatch an angel to stop the slaughter in Europe. Had Jews done more *teshuva*, perhaps that angel might have been dispatched. What we do know is that we are never bereft of choices. No matter who we are, no matter what situation we find ourselves in, we can always choose to dedicate our lives to serving *Hashem* as a tzevaos. The choice is holocaust or *teshuva*. And it is a good sign that not long after the destruction of European Jewry, we have been witness to this world-wide Jewish reawakening to the truths of the Torah.

As we move on in the time period the prophets called the End of Days[106] — the climax of history as we know it — the light of Torah begins to filter into the world. This light is the original light that *Hashem* created and stored away for the future.

> And *Hashem* said, "Let there be light," and there was light. And *Hashem* saw that the light was good; and *Hashem* divided (*vayavdail*) between the light and the darkness. (*Beraishis* 1:3,4)

To this, Rashi (basing himself on the words of *Chazal*) comments:

> *Hashem* saw that the wicked were unworthy of using the light. He therefore set it apart (*vayavdail*) from them and hid it away for the righteous in the world-to-come.
>
> According to the simple meaning, though, explain it as follows: *Hashem* saw that the light was good and it was therefore not proper that it should exist side by side (*b'eervuviah*) with the darkness. He therefore limited one's sphere of activity to daytime and one's sphere of activity to nighttime.

Light and darkness, as we see them today, are not able to exist side by side (i.e. independently and yet concurrently). To us, in fact, the entire idea seems impossible and preposterous. When it is dark, there is no light. When it is light, there is no darkness. Even twilight is nothing more than a *mixture* of light and darkness. Some light gives way to some darkness. The two do not exist side by side, though, without one effecting the other.

However, Rashi tells us, the nature of the original light which *Hashem* "hid" away was a light which could not be pushed away by darkness; the original light and darkness that *Hashem* created did exist concurrently, side by side (*b'eervuviah*). To us, for both to actually exist concurrently defies rationality. Nevertheless, the original light did defy rationality. *Hashem* hid that original light and set it aside for the righteous in the future. He replaced it with a light and darkness whose properties included being *unable* to exist concurrently.

Rashi tells us that *Hashem* hid this original light. Where did He hide it?

Light is a metaphor for wisdom, knowledge, Torah. (In fact, the physical world — including its light — was created as an afterthought to Torah. "*Hashem* looked into the Torah and created the world."[107]) Where did He hide that original light? He hid it in the Torah, the source of wisdom and knowledge of *Hashem*.

As the arrival of the Messianic age looms closer, the original light will begin to shine forth little by little. In our own times, over recent decades, we have seen this presence of a new light — the original light. For instance, the trend toward assimilation, when it first began some two hundred years ago, proved that light could not exist in the face of darkness. Torah and atheism could not coexist without one pushing the other away. And, of course, until fifty years ago at least, atheism (Communism in the East and secular materialism in the West) was clearly winning.

However, things have changed. The Jewish world is now witness to the Teshuva Movement. This is an unprecedented return of Jews previously isolated in the darkest darkness of estrangement from Torah, who somehow sensed the light present in their heritage, in their very hearts. In the Teshuva phenomenon we clearly see the influence of the new light, one which cannot be pushed away by darkness. In the same secular family, often one child has returned to the ways of Torah while his or her siblings have moved to the other extreme and even intermarried. That suggests that the light the *baal teshuva* sees emanates from a point hidden within himself that does not get pushed aside in the face of darkness.

The first hint of the entrance of this new light in the modern era was the Holocaust, which, paradoxically, was the darkest of darknesses.

Hitler epitomized the darkness which could not coexist with light. Thus, he opposed the light with all his might. And for a while it seemed as if he had won.

Then, at the last moment, when he seemed to have blacked out the Jew's light entirely, he uncovered something that had been hiding until then: the eternal, original light. Despite his half-decade reign of world dominance, he could not extinguish the Jewish light. The story of the *baal teshuva* Mattisyahu and his disciples, the Bais Yaakov girls, the Jewish boys who danced on *Simchas Torah*, the woman arriving at the concentration camp who wanted nothing more than to circumcise her newborn, the simple chicken farmer locked in the cattle car with his dying family — and many, many others — revealed the one-of-a-kind light that pulses in every Jewish soul.

When the light of a candle is snuffed out, and yet light remains, one must conclude that there is an alternate source of light. That is what Hitler did in effect. He engulfed the old light in his darkness. However, a light still remained, revealing the existence of an alternate light source, the new light. When the Jewish people emerged from the worst of Nazi-imposed tribulations with their light still shining, it was clear that the light retained was (and is) not the secondary light which can be pushed away by darkness. It was (and is) an intrinsic light, a light that is eternal.

Thus, the Holocaust can help the contemporary Jew uncover the hidden light within himself. Hitler inaugurated a new era. Before Hitler, we were living with a light that could be countered by darkness. Since his time, a new light has begun filtering into the world. This is the light of the era of the Third *Bais HaMikdash*. This is the light we refer to today in our prayers every day when we say, *ohr chodosh al tzion ta'ir*, "a new light will shine on Zion."

Imagine a dark tunnel. As one enters and travels further, the light from the entrance grows dimmer and dimmer. There is a second light, though, a light at the other end of the tunnel, at the exit. That light does not immediately reach the one who is approaching from the entrance. It does not reach him until he comes to the darkest point in the tunnel, the point furthest removed from the entrance light and preceding infiltration of the exit light.

This is a metaphor of Jewish history.

The entrance light is the light emanating from the revelation at Mount Sinai (represented by Moshe and the *matan Torah*, the giving of the Torah). As we moved away from that event and entered the darkness of exile, the light from Mount Sinai became dimmer and dimmer. Jewish history is filled with dark chapters. However, the darkest chapter was the Holocaust. It was just after that darkest point, however, that the light from the exit (represented by Rebbi Akiva and *kabbolas HaTorah*, the receiving of Torah) first began to radiate. This new light does not shine all at once; but steadily and slowly grows greater and greater, brighter and brighter, bit by bit.

The Holocaust is intimately connected to the era of the Third *Bais HaMikdash*, to the original light which *Hashem* hid away for the righteous in the future. We can say with confidence that light is slowly beginning to filter into our world because our greatest experience of darkness proved that our light can never be extinguished. That was the Holocaust. It was from that extreme blackness that the deepest, most essential light of the Jew — of the Yisroel within — came out of hiding.

This theme is dramatically portrayed in the story of a baptized Jew in pre-war Poland. A convert to Christianity, he rose in status until he became mayor of his town. As was the norm with such Jews, he promulgated decrees against his Jewish brethren without mercy, becoming one of the worst anti-semites.

War came. The Nazis occupied his town and deported all its Jews. The gestapo eventually heard a rumor that the mayor was really a Jew who had converted to Christianity. They summoned him and asked him if he was a Jew. He could easily have denied it; after all, he probably considered himself a Christian. However, for some reason he neither denied nor confirmed their allegation.

Their questions became increasingly intense until the ordeal took the form of an interrogation. Through it all, he refused to speak. Finally, they decided to test his allegiance. They brought him to a synagogue, took out a Torah scroll, put it into his hands, and told him to throw it to the floor and step on it.

"If you do that," they told him, "you have proven to us that you are not a Jew."

As he held the Torah, he burst out in joy and exclaimed, "Thank you, Germans. You have given me back my Judaism. I threw it away, but now you have given it back to me." With that statement, he went to his death.

This Jew had been a traitor of the highest order who persecuted his brethren. How could such a Jew face death with such Jewish nobility and courage? The answer is: a Jew's essence can never be besmirched. When the

Germans told him to strip away his Jewish identity to the core — precisely at that moment — his Jewish soul burst forth. The night had reached its darkest point, and all that was left was the *ohr chodosh*, the new light. This was the way the Nazis turned Jews, who otherwise would have been completely lost (to their people as well as themselves), into *kodoshim*, holy ones.

In our post-Holocaust world, the alternative path still exists and beckons us to travel down it. A Jew who is like a ram of the forest can rediscover what it means to be part of the *tzevaos* of *Hashem*. And that is the challenge in the post-Holocaust world. How can we change ourselves from rams for the slaughter into fervent bearers of the mission inherent in the name Yisroel? That is the most important question for the Jewish people today. Our very generation's survival depends upon answering that question. And that is what we aim to accomplish in the next chapter.

CHAPTER 7

REBBI AKIVA

The 2,000 years of *yimos HaMoshiach* — these past two millennia of suffering and exile — are characterized most by Rebbi Akiva (as we elaborated upon earlier).[108]

Akiva ben Yosef was a descendant of converts. At forty years of age he was ignorant of Torah and vehemently antagonistic toward its scholars. One day, he made a monumental decision to study Torah. However, he met with obstacles.

He felt dull-witted and inadequate, overwhelmed ready to quit. Then he chanced by a cave and saw a rock with a hole bored through it. The hole had been created by the continuous dripping of water from a point above. At that moment he thought to himself, "If water, which is soft, is able to bore a hole in a rock, which is hard, then certainly the words of Torah, which are hard, can bore a hole through my heart."[109]

That moment of *self*-knowledge was momentous not only for him but for the Jewish people. From that day onward, he never stopped learning. He grew so great that he not only became the leader of his generation but the light for all of the ensuing dark generations of exile.

Rebbi Akiva's Torah

The *Gemara* relates just how great Rebbi Akiva's achievement was, and just how much it meant for future generations:[110]

> When Moshe went up to heaven to receive the Torah, he saw *Hashem* [had not yet finished the Torah, but was still busy] decorating the letters of the Torah with crowns (*k'sarim*). Moshe said, "*Hashem*, who delayed Your finishing the Torah?"
>
> "There is a person," *Hashem* answered, "who will live at the end of certain generations [i.e. some time in the future]. Akiva the son of Yosef is his name. He will be able to deduce from *kol kots v'kots* 'each and every point' [of the letters in the Torah] mountains and mountains of *halachos*."
>
> "Please, show me this person," Moshe asked.
>
> "Go [prophetically] to his generation."
>
> Moshe did so. He went to the yeshiva where Rebbi Akiva taught, and sat in a seat at the end of the eighth row.

However, he could not understand the lesson. He felt weak, embarrassed. Finally, the lecture reached a point where the disciples asked Rebbi Akiva, "How do you know this?"

Rebbi Akiva answered: "*Halacha l'Moshe m'Sinai*, we received the law from Sinai through Moshe."

Moshe felt comforted. However, he said to *Hashem*, "If you have such a great person as this Akiva, why are You giving the Torah through me? You should give it through Rebbi Akiva."

"Ask no more," *Hashem* said. "This came up in My thoughts."

Moshe then asked, "*Hashem*, You have shown me the extent of his Torah knowledge. Now, please show me his *schar*." [The usual translation of *schar* is "reward." However, the word can also be translated as "price." Thus, instead of asking *Hashem* to show him Rebbi Akiva's reward, we can render Moshe's request to be: What price does it cost to become a Rebbi Akiva? How much does one have to pay in order to merit possessing the Torah greatness of Rebbi Akiva?]

"Go to his generation," *Hashem* said.

[In the days of Rebbi Akiva, the Romans had conquered Judea and were attempting to snuff out all remnants of Jewish pride and identity. They forbade the teaching of Torah on threat of public execution. Rebbi Akiva openly disobeyed the decree, citing his famous parable of the fox and the fish wherein the fox says to the fish:

"Fish, fishermen are just upstream ready to catch you. Come up here on the shore where it is safe."

"Fool," said the fish, "if I am not safe in water, which is

my natural habitat, then I will certainly not be safe on land!"

So, too, Rebbi Akiva reasoned to his compatriots: if a Jew is not safe immersed in Torah, which is to him like water to the fish, then how much more in danger is he if he abandons the Torah, his natural habitat? (*Berachos* 61b)

The Romans imprisoned Rebbi Akiva and eventually brought him out for public execution. They chose an especially cruel execution: combing his flesh with steel. As his soul was about to leave him, at the height of his suffering, Rebbi Akiva told his disciples that he had always waited for this moment, for he had always worried how he would ever be able to fulfill the words of Torah which tell one to love *Hashem* 'with all your heart, with all your soul, and with all your might.' Now, however, as they tore away his flesh, the moment had come and it was enabling him to finally unearth the deepest yearnings for *Hashem* his noble soul could muster. Finally, as his soul departed, he said, *Shma Yisroel Hashem Elokeinu Hashem Echod*, "Hear Israel, *Hashem* is our *Hashem*, *Hashem* is one."]

Moshe went to the days of Rebbi Akiva and saw that the flesh of his [Rebbi Akiva's] body was weighed on a butcher's scale. Moshe asked, "Master of the Universe, this is the Torah and this is its *schar,* its price?"

"Ask no more," *Hashem* told him once again. "This came up in My thoughts."

Everything about Rebbi Akiva contains a particularly special lesson for us living during the era of *yimos HaMoshiach*. Thus, the above passage, is remarkable not only what it teaches us about Rebbi Akiva, but for what it teaches us about ourselves. To begin explaining it, we must recall something we learned earlier.

There are two distinct historical eras with two distinct types of Torah. One is the 2,000 years of Torah — the Torah of Moshe — and the other is the 2,000 years of *yimos HaMoshiach* — the Torah of Rebbi Akiva. In reality, of course, there is only one unchanging Torah. However, different circumstances tend to highlight the different ways Torah living can be expressed. For instance, the Torah lifestyle in medieval Europe manifested itself differently from the Torah lifestyle in the times of the *Bais HaMikdash*. Thus, although there is only one Torah with 613 commandments, nevertheless, the nuances in which that Torah is expressed vary from time to time and place to place.

The difference between the Torah of Moshe and the Torah of Rebbi Akiva is significant. It is the difference between the Torah performed under optimal conditions versus the Torah performed under less than optimal conditions. It is the difference between the Torah of sovereignty in the land and the Torah of exile. It is the difference between Torah which is given (*matan* Torah) and Torah which is received (*kabbolas* Torah).

The Torah of Moshe is the Torah given through miracles and prophecy. That Torah, in essence, is *Hashem*'s doing; it is the Torah given on Sinai through Moshe (which is represented by the Hebrew letters in the Torah scroll). The Torah of Rebbi Akiva, on the other hand, is the Torah received through exile and suffering. That Torah is written with one's own sweat and blood (and is represented by the *k'sarim,* "crowns," of the letters).

"The *halachos* which [*Hashem* told Moshe that] Rebbi Akiva would deduce" is a reference to the idea that significantly different external circumstances would exist between Moshe's time and Rebbi Akiva's time. These circumstances would perforce raise new *halachic* questions which would require authentic Torah responses — responses that could only come from someone who grasped the Torah principles at their core, like Moshe.

That someone was Rebbi Akiva. When people came and asked him how to deal with a specific problem in Torah law, raised by the circumstances of living under the oppressive Roman authorities, he plummeted into the depths of Torah and deduced the authentic *halacha.* His depth of understanding extended so far that he was able to "deduce" this novel yet authentic application of *halacha* even from the tiny points which formed the shape of the Hebrew letters.

The Hebrew word for "a point" (of a letter in the Torah), *kots*, also means pinpoint or needle. Thus, the phrase in the passage which reads: "from each and every point (*kol kots v'kots)*, [Rebbi Akiva will] deduce mountains and mountains of *halachos*" can be understood: from each and every "needling" — with every pang of suffering and pain that he and the people of his time experience — Rebbi Akiva will deduce *halachos.* He will bring to light an authentic Torah of exile, a Torah which existed in potential from Moshe's time but was first actualized by Rebbi Akiva.

On a deeper level, the Torah scrolls in our *shuls* and synagogues are more than mere holy words on parchment. They are the physical counterpart of a great spiritual Torah, and each Jew parallels a different letter. We are taught that the 600,000 letters in the Torah parallel the 600,000 Jews who stood at Mount Sinai.[111] This is true for all ensuing generations as well. Each person in each generation corresponds to a letter in that spiritual Torah. And when *Moshiach* comes each of us will know exactly which letter we were.

Moshe's Torah consisted of the basic forms of the Hebrew letters. Rebbi Akiva's Torah, though, adds extra crowns (*k'sarim*) which beautify the Torah. The idea is as follows: One who is merely given the Torah (i.e. one who acquires his spot in the spiritual Torah without effort, struggle, or suffering) will have a relatively plain and unadorned personal letter. Only one who earns Torah as Rebbi Akiva did, through the strain of making oneself a hollowed receptacle for Torah (*kabbolas* Torah), beautifies his letter with crowns. Beautification of one's letter in the spiritual Torah results only from overcoming adversity. Indeed, the greater the adversity, the greater the beauty.

That was epitomized by Rebbi Akiva. He rebuilt and reprogrammed his entire outlook on life. He trained himself to see the good where others saw only bad. The *Gemara* recounts the story of when Rebbi Akiva and several other sages were passing by the ruins of the *Bais HaMikdash* and saw a fox scurry out from amongst the ruins. While the sages wept, Rebbi Akiva laughed. They asked him how he could possibly laugh at such a sight. He explained, "Now that I see exactly how the prophecies concerning the destruction have come to full fruition, I see all the more how the parallel prophecies concerning the ultimate redemption will come to fruition." To this, the sages replied, "Akiva, you have comforted us."[112]

Rebbi Akiva acquired the underpinnings of his outlook from his early teacher, a sage named Nachum Ish Gamzu.[113] His name extended from the fact that he would always say, "*GAM ZU l'tovah*," "this too is for the good," no matter how bleak a situation looked. The ability to turn adversity into gain, perhaps the most basic ingredient in Rebbi Akiva's outlook on life, was nowhere more poignantly articulated than in his death.

Of course, Rebbi Akiva's brutal death is not easily understood by us (just as it was not easily understood by Moshe, as the *Gemara* cited previously informed us). Nevertheless, to Rebbi Akiva, it was not perplexing. He told his disciples, "I have waited my entire life for this." His entire life was spent converting the gloom of adversity into the exhilaration of triumph. He had waited his entire life for the ultimate adversity so that he could produce the ultimate triumph. That is why the finale to his magnificent life was not a tragic moment for him, but a moment he had yearned his whole life for.

This is what the *Gemara* means when it says that Moshe saw Rebbi Akiva's flesh on a scale of a butcher shop and then asked, "Is this his *schar*?" A scale weighs one thing against another. You give meat. You get money. Flesh represents the comfort of materialism. Rebbi Akiva's *schar*, the price he paid for his Torah, was his entire material existence. As they combed his flesh with steel, it was as if they were weighing every morsel of his material, physical existence and exchanging it for the priceless spiritual wealth of Torah. And when Rebbi Akiva uttered his last word, *echod*, he literally became "one" with *Hashem*; he had divested himself of all material impediments that normally exist between creation and Creator, and thus became one with *Hashem*.

Generally speaking, a person is not allowed to ask for suffering nor may he seek ways to bring more suffering upon himself. (See Question 11 in Appendix.) However, when suffering is thrust upon us we must know that it is an opportunity for more than "overcoming" — it is an opportunity to attain the heights of achievement. Of course, this is a high ideal (and that is why the judicious person does not ask for suffering). Nevertheless, when one realizes what stands to be gained with a moment of suffering, then he can clear his mind and focus only on the great reward that will ultimately accrue. That awareness blocks out even tremendous pain.

This *Gemara's* lesson is for the individual who suffers like a Rebbi Akiva: Every pang which results from an unbearable situation sent down upon us from above, comes to us along with the choice to convert that pang into spiritual achievement. That is the process of beautification of our personal letter in the great spiritual Torah.

More significantly, the ultimate redemption is dependent upon our ability to beautify our letter. Moshe's Torah constitutes the letters; Rebbi Akiva's Torah represents the beautification — and the *Gemara* informed us that *Hashem* was delayed completing the spiritual Torah only by the latter's part in the process, the placement of *k'sarim,* the crowns which beautify Torah. Thus, it is incumbent upon us to view every personal holocaust which *Hashem* weaves into our lives as an opportunity for personal redemption, as well as an opportunity to bring about the redemption of the world. Each successful imitation of Akiva's achievement brings the spiritual Torah another step closer toward completion.

Open Marriage, Closed Heart

Rebbi Akiva is the inspiration for those of us living during the 2,000 years of *yimos HaMoshiach*. Even in the comfort of modern Western society, opportunities to "beautify the [spiritual] Torah" abound. And there are many stories of "miniature" Rebbi Akivas. One involves a young man raised in an affluent home.

His parents, both psychologists, had little knowledge of Judaism. Their son had even less. Although he had hitch-hiked and explored almost half the globe, he had never been to the land of his people. Eventually, though, he decided to "make a stop" even there.

At the Wailing Wall, he was invited to attend a class at one of the local yeshivas, Ohr Somayach. He accepted the invitation, attended a lecture, and then a second lecture. The wisdom, the rapport between students and teachers all — relatively quickly — "turned him on." For the first time in his life, he realized that his own heritage contained answers to questions he had always wondered about but never knew how to approach. He stayed one day and then another and then another. In time, he became totally committed to Torah Judaism.

He wrote a letter to his parents explaining how he had found something so meaningful. His parents wrote back, "Son, as long as you are happy, we are happy. As long as you don't tell us what to do, we won't tell you what to do. We're very supportive. The main thing is: be happy."

Unfortunately, to the parents' way of thinking, it could

have been a cult. It did not matter that it was Judaism their son had rediscovered. As long as he was happy.

The young man stayed in Israel with his parents' consent and support. He continued his studies there for the next fourteen months. One day, he received a letter from his parents with a round-trip ticket. They wanted to see him. "Come home for a month," they said, "and then go back."

At first, he was reluctant. His parents did not observe *Shabbos,* did not eat *kosher* food, nor did they keep anything else in the Torah. He did not know how he could maintain his observance isolated in their home. He talked to his teachers and finally to the head of the yeshiva, who told him, "Listen, the Torah commands you to 'Honor your father and mother.' Of course, they don't really understand what you are all about now. Nevertheless, they are supportive of you, and they have a right to ask you to come home to see them. They love you. You have to go home."

"But what about *Shabbos*?" he asked.

"*Shabbos*? Make *Shabbos* yourself and invite them to join you."

"What about *kashrus*?"

"Set up a little *kosher* kitchen for yourself. You can manage. Go home and share what you have learned with them."

He went home. About a week later, I bumped into this young man at the Yeshiva Ohr Somayach branch in

Monsey, New York, and remembered I had met him at Ohr Somayach in Jerusalem several months earlier. He had been a vibrant young man; now, however, he was pale as could be, and seemed on the verge of collapse.

"Is anything wrong?" I asked.

"Well, I have a few questions on *halacha*," he said.

We went into the office and sat down with one of the heads of the yeshiva, Rabbi Yisroel Rokowsky. The boy presented his questions.

"When I left my house fourteen months ago, my parents had a great relationship. As far back as I remember, they always loved each other. But while I was away these fourteen months, my parents felt that their lives lacked excitement. So, they began experimenting with this open marriage concept. To make a long story short, my father met another woman, a non-Jew, and my mother met a non-Jewish man. They have decided to divorce and remarry these others.

"'Why not?' they asked me. The fun had come to an end. They needed some new excitement in their lives. They harbored no hard feelings toward each other. In fact, not only did they begin divorce proceedings very civilly, but they even purposely arranged to remarry their new partners a week apart from each other. And since they are very open-minded people, they wanted me to attend both weddings. That is why they asked me to come home.

"All this was going on while I was in Israel," he said.

"They knew that if they had written me the real reason they wanted me to come home, I might have refused. So they omitted this information in their letter. Only now have I found out about the situation.

"I've fallen apart," he admitted with tears rolling down his face. "I love my mother and father, and they still like each other. They have no bad feelings about one another. It's only that life became too dry for them."

He regained his composure and said, "After they informed me of these happenings, they asked me what I felt.

"'What do I feel?' I said, 'My mother and father, who still like each other, are getting a divorce, breaking up the family, and now you want to know how I feel?! Why didn't you think about my feelings before you came to this decision?'

"'We don't understand why you are so upset,' they countered. 'You do what you like. We do what we like. You enjoy yourself living in the yeshiva. We enjoy ourselves living the way we do.'

"I tried to talk them out of it, but there's no use. They have made up their minds and can't change merely because of my feelings. They intend to go through with the arrangements.

"Now, my question to you is the," the young man said. "My mother just asked me to help her move all of her personal belongings from my father's house and take them into her boyfriend's house. This is very difficult for me. I despise being there. However, what does the *halacha* say? Does it forbid me to do it because I would be helping her transgress the prohibition of intermarriage. Or, perhaps, the *halacha* does allow me to do it, in which case I have to do it despite my feelings because of the commandment to honor my mother and father.

"The second question is: This *Shabbos,* my father is throwing a barbecue for his girlfriend. If my father asks me to bring out the meat, many problems arise. First, the meat is non-*kosher*; second, it is forbidden to barbecue anything on *Shabbos*; third, I'm not allowed to carry it because there is no *eruv*; and fourth, the whole party is for his non-Jewish fiancee. What am I allowed to do and what am I not allowed to do? I am ready to do whatever the *halacha* demands."

It is really not relevant for the purpose of this book to explain everything we recommended to the young man. But when this young man left the office, both Rabbi Rokowsky and I sat dumbfounded and looked at each other for a moment. Then I said emotionally, "Look, we Jewish people have the richest library in the history of the world. Volumes and volumes, covering all kinds of questions over thousands of years, have been recorded. Everything is well-documented. However, find me a question like that!"

(This, by the way, is a perfect illustration of the *Gemara* quoted previously — when it says Moshe did not understand the Torah of Rebbi Akiva. When Torah is given from above, as it was to Moshe, this type of question does not arise. Only in the era of Rebbi Akiva, when Torah is taken away from us and we have to deal with the Torah of exile, do such questions of *halacha* arise.)

We sat quietly a moment longer and then I added, "Find me such an unbelievable young man. Not even a year and a half ago he knew absolutely nothing about his heritage. Now, he comes to his rabbi asking detailed questions, in all sincerity, concerning the laws of honoring his father and mother. And he is willing to do whatever the Torah tells him to do, despite his personal feelings.

"If this boy had not become observant, and his mother and father made such requests of him, wouldn't he have slammed the door in their faces or flung profanities them? But now that he has become a man of Torah, as painful as it is to him he is ready to accept whatever the Torah decrees. He dares to ask questions which go against his own desires and wishes.

"Materialism and man-made systems of thought have distorted the minds of even the most good-hearted people today. It is one thing to see Jews who care nothing about Torah and step on its principles. However, it is an entirely different matter to bear witness to a generation of Jewish parents who view themselves as the height of the civilized humanistic world, who at the same time show no concern for the emotions of their own son!

They divorce not because they cannot bear to live with one another, but to have a little bit of a better time. This was unheard of fifty years ago. Our grandparents may have lacked the trappings of civilization, but they were totally self-sacrificing for their loved ones and the things that mattered most."

To comfort the young man, I invited him to my house for *Shabbos* and at one of the meals I shared with him a teaching of Rabbi Tzadok HaCohen[114] (who flourished about 120 years ago). Rabbi Tzadok wrote that over the entire course of history, three generations will stand out: the Generation of the Flood (*Mabul*), the Generation in the Desert (*Midbar*), and the generation in which *Moshiach* will arrive.

The Generation of the Flood will stand out in terms of wickedness. They did everything for lust, for personal pleasure; as the verse says about them, "All flesh has corrupted its way."[115]

The Generation of the Desert was the diametric opposite: they were outstanding in righteousness. It was they who stood at Mount Sinai and received the Torah; it was they who gave up everything and followed *Hashem* into the desert to fulfill Torah and *mitzvos.*

Rabbi Tzadok wrote that the generation before *Moshiach's* coming will reexperience both the Generation of the Flood and the Generation of the Desert simultaneously. And both will vie for leadership in an all-out battle to the death. In the end, the Generation of the

Desert will overcome the Generation of the Flood, Rabbi Tzadok writes, and that will bring *Moshiach.*

I concluded by telling this young man, "I know many young people of the Generation of the Desert who have brothers or sisters who have married out of the fold. However, who would have thought that parents from the Generation of the Flood will give birth to children from the Generation of the Desert?. Although your parents are not to blame (because they themselves were only the by-product of Jews who abandoned Torah due to unbearable persecution), nevertheless, they are of the Generation of the Flood. You are from the Generation of the Desert. You are fighting for Torah, and not just passively, but in a way where you earn every ounce of Torah you possess."

Rebbi Akiva's Great Principle

A Roman citizen once approached the great sage, Hillel, and asked him, "Teach me the entire Torah while standing on one foot" (i.e. as succinctly as possible.)

Hillel responded. "Do not do unto others as you would not want them to do unto you. That is the whole Torah. The rest is commentary."[116]

In actuality, Hillel told him that the verse, "Love thy neighbor as yourself," is the foundation of the Torah. (Hillel merely reformulated it in the negative.) Rebbi Akiva came along and stated this outright: *v'ohavta l'reiyacha komocha, zeh klal gadol baTorah*, "Love your neighbor as yourself — this is the great principle of the Torah."

Rebbi Akiva emphasized an aspect of this verse that was not well understood. He saw that people tended to emphasize the first two words, *v'ohavta l'reiyacha*, "Love your neighbor." However, Rebbi Akiva wanted to stress that the foundation of the verse is the third word, *komocha,* "like yourself." If one does not first love oneself, then there can be no real love of another. And thus, *ahavas Yisroel,* love of a fellow Jew, is first dependent upon the love of the Yisroel in oneself.

In this, Rebbi Akiva is consistent with another statement he made. The *Gemara* discusses a case where two people are stranded in the desert with enough water for only one of them to survive. Although one sage says that they should split the water even though that would inevitably lead to both of their deaths, Rebbi Akiva disagrees. He maintains that a person first has an obligation to save himself. According to Rebbi Akiva, the one who has the water canteen should use the water in order to save himself. Thus, through this legal decision, we see again that the central idea of Rebbi Akiva's entire approach is the self. To him, it is the foundation of the great principle of the Torah.

One should not think that this principle of self is a form of selfishness. The source of Jewish sense of self is awareness of oneself as part of the *om kodosh*, the holy nation. The Jewish people were created as an *om kodosh*; they have been put on this earth to represent *Hashem* and to bring the world to its destined completed state. Only this type of Jewish self-dignity, self-pride, and self-love produces beneficial results.

The *Mishnah* tells us: "All Yisroel has a portion in the world to come."[117] At its root, this means that each Jew has an irreplaceable role in transforming the world-as-it-is into the world-to-come. If your job in a car construction project is to make the spark plugs, and you do not do your job, then the final car will not run despite the fact that everyone else did their job. If a Jew is not doing his part in bringing about the purpose of creation, then that purpose will not be reached. And no other Jew can replace him. He has an irreplaceable role in the overall plan. Thus, it all starts with ourselves. We have to discover our particular, unique role and perform it to the best of our ability. If we do not, then everyone else will be lacking. In this regard, the *Mishnah* stated: "Every Yisroel has an [irreplaceable] role in [bringing about] the world to come."

Jewish sense of self is founded upon viewing oneself as a vital part on the *om kodosh*, performing the Creator's needs in this world. No one else can do what you were created to do. This is what Hillel meant when he said, "If I am not for myself, who will be?"[118] No one else will do it for you. And that is what Rebbi Akiva meant when he said that *komocha,* the principle of self, is the great principle in the Torah.

The Foundation

The truth is that there are other great principles in the Torah. In fact, Judaism is specifically built upon three major principles: *Hashem*, Torah, and Yisroel (i.e. the Jew).[119] Even in this regard, however, Rebbi Akiva's aphorism that the Yisroel-self is the foundation of Torah applies.

Generally, a building has three parts: the foundation, the structure itself, and the roof (which is like a crown to the entire building). So, too, the building of Judaism has three parts. *Hashem* is the crown. Torah is the structure. And Yisroel is the foundation. If a building's foundation should crumble, everything else will fall. So, too, regarding Judaism. Should the foundation — the fundamental belief of Yisroel — crumble, the entire structure will not stand. The restoration of this world to its destined status is dependent upon Yisroel — Yisroel who becomes one with Torah and strives ever upward toward unity with *Hashem*.

This also explains a question people often have. During the 2,000 years of Torah, we seemed to have had everything: open miracles (i.e. *Hashem*) and Torah. If the Jewish people were not able to complete their mission when they had everything, then how can one expect them to complete it when they have nothing?

The answer is that although we had *Hashem* and Torah, we did not really have Yisroel. The *komocha* was missing.

How could that be? The answer is that when we thought we had everything — our *Bais HaMikdash*, our kings, our *Sanhedrin*, our culture, our land, our army, our standing in the world — we neglected ourselves. We pinned our self-worth on visible manifestations. However, in doing so, we took for granted the most sublime essence: the Yisroel, the part of *Hashem* on high beating in our own breast. That essence is the foundation — the unchanging, unalterable foundation.

When the Jewish people lost everything — the manifestations of *Hashem* and Torah in their life — it looked like the bleakest of times. Nothing was left. Absolutely nothing. However, with Jews there is never really nothing left. No matter how much else gets stripped away, there "was, is, and always will be" that indestructible essence: Yisroel. "All Yisroel has a portion in the world to come" and each one is a letter in the spiritual Torah. Neither the portion in the world to come nor the letter in the spiritual Torah can ever be lost. (Only one's distinction of having worked for and earned that portion or that letter can be lost.) Thus, paradoxically, when everything else is lost, one can sometimes more easily rediscover the foundation, the *komocha.* And from there everything else can be rebuilt.

It is especially appropriate that Rebbi Akiva should be the one credited with teaching the great principle of the Torah, because he epitomized starting with nothing. He was a descendant of one of the most wicked men to ever live — Sisera — and was illiterate until the age of forty. Stripped of everything else, he could not attach self-worth to any external manifestation of his essence. Yet he knew that he was a Jew. Thus, as naked as he was of the externals of a Jewish being, Rebbi Akiva did not neglect appreciating his self — his Yisroel. And it was this ability to recognize the value of his Yisroel self that eventually gave him the foundation to soar far above his peers.

The Three Principles in our Times

These three principles — *Hashem*, Torah, and Yisroel — are destined to come to bear in the generation before *Moshiach* to a greater degree than ever before, because that generation will have to become imbued with them more than any other generation. And over the past fifty years, one can see that the Jewish people have indeed been going through three corresponding types of tests.

The first was the Holocaust. which tested the first principle: belief in *Hashem*. *Hashem* did everything to test us. Only those who continued to believe in *Hashem* after the Holocaust passed this test. Unfortunately, many could not withstand the test, and had the roof of their structure of Judaism wiped away.

Almost immediately after the Holocaust, the State of Israel was declared and established. It was the first time in history that the Jewish people were given the chance to express pride about being a Jew *without* Torah. Until then, Jewish pride was expressed keeping *Hashem*'s Torah. "[You] chose us from all the nations and gave us the Torah."[120] "For it [the Torah] is your wisdom in the eyes of the nations."[121] Without Torah, we had nothing to be proud of in the eyes of the world. We were people in exile for 2,000 years, lacking a homeland. Our entire source of self-dignity as Jews was the Torah.

What did *Hashem* do? He gave us a tremendous test. He gave us our own State — a secular State — with our own army — a victorious army. In the beginning of the statehood, all the nations respected the Jews for making the land of Israel fertile once more and conquering all their enemies. Jews could raise their heads as secular Jews, walk into the United Nations, become ambassadors around the world, and declare proudly: We are Jews . . . *without* the Torah.

A Jewish State has been established without mentioning the name of *Hashem*. It is a state of law, based more on principles of British law, rather than a state based on *halacha,* the foundation of Jewish law. This is the first opportunity of its kind in all Jewish history. And the question *Hashem* is asking the Jewish people is: Are you proud because you have Torah, or are you proud because you now have a bureaucracy like all other nations?

Those who continue to know that without Torah we are nothing, have withstood this test. Those who do not know are like a foundation without a structure.

Now, during these final days, we are undergoing the third test: the *komocha,* the test to find the Yisroel in ourselves, and loving it. And a person cannot do that unless he appreciates what Yisroel is. Yisroel is in this world to represent *Hashem*, to fulfill Torah, from its smallest detail to its greatest principle, so that as one perfectly integrated whole, we can all bring the purpose of creation to fruition. Loving oneself or another Jew for some other reasons is shallow and ultimately self-destructive.

Those who pass the third test will be able to love their neighbors and themselves even when they are in the lowest of positions, devoid (seemingly) of everything of worth. Those who cannot stand up to this test, will join the ranks of those Jews whose pillars of Judaism teeter on a weak foundation. For the members of this latter group, the loss of everything is the mechanism of change. Sooner or later, from within or from without, they will realize that they have nothing left but the fact that they are Jews. From that self-knowledge they will have the impetus necessary to dig a proper foundation and rebuild the entire structure up to the crown itself.

Rebbi Akiva's Great Moment

Now we can return to gain a deeper understanding of Rebbi Akiva's final act. The Yisroel in oneself is found sometimes only when that Yisroel self is concealed in the deepest of darknesses. For forty years of his own life,

Rebbi Akiva drowned in darkness. Yet, he became the light of Torah for his generation and, in fact, for all the generations of the Jewish people's darkest exile.

Then, at the end of his life, when he was brought into the public to be executed — at the height of pain, suffering, and darkness — he uttered with tranquility and dignity the battlecry of the Jew, the *Shma Yisroel.* It was as if he was telling his disciples (and all of us who have read their description of the account), "Perhaps you thought my greatness centered upon some noble human capacity like intelligence or perseverance. Those are indeed noble. But when they are literally stripped away and you see that I am mortal like yourselves, that I am a flesh and blood creature, then you must realize that the inner greatness of a Jew extends not from anything dependent upon human nature. It is an inner absolute source. An intrinsic source. It is the *ohr chodosh,*[122] the new, original light which shines forever.

"I am teaching you this my dear, beloved disciples because once you know that clearly, then you can tap into your own *ohr chodosh*; you can begin to go about your daily work for *Hashem* fueled by that intrinsic source, not by the old, extrinsic source. Therefore, do not look upon the superficialities of my predicament now. (Neither look upon the superficialities of your own predicament.) Although you look at me and think you see the darkest of darknesses, it is in this very moment of blackness that I am burning with the brightest of lights. Bathe in my light and learn how to radiate it yourself.

"Hear this Yisroel — the Yisroel in yourself — and let the words echo in your ears until the *ohr chodosh al tzion ta'ir*, until "the new light will shine on Zion" — *Hashem* is our *Hashem*, *Hashem* is One."

Conclusion

Dear Reader, I would like to conclude with words of consolation for you. Everything here is directly applicable to the individual who suffers. There is no end to the amount the individual can learn from the suffering of the whole Jewish people. No matter what troubled and hopeless situation you find yourself in, you can derive great consolation from understanding what you are accomplishing with your suffering.

When *Hashem* first sent Moshe to Pharaoh and told him, "Let my people go," Pharaoh responded by worsening the oppression to the point where the Jews complained to Moshe, "Ever since you arrived, things have gotten much worse."[123]

Moshe returned to *Hashem* and said, "Why did You make it worse for this nation? Why have You sent me? Ever since I came to Pharaoh to speak in Your name it has become much worse for the people."

Hashem responded, "I am *Hashem*. Whenever I appeared to Avraham, Yitzchak, and Yaakov I revealed Myself as (*Kail Shakai*) the 'Almighty.' But My name

Havayah (the four letter name of *Hashem*) I did not reveal to them."

How did *Hashem's* words answer Moshe's question?

There are two ways in which *Hashem* runs the world: through nature and through special intervention. The natural world is developed with the name *Kail Shakai*, the Almighty. *Shakai* means "enough" or limitation. The natural world by definition is a limitation of *Hashem*'s essence because it runs in a natural way — a way that, superficially at least, seems to have a course of its own.

On the other hand, the name *Havayah* means that *Hashem* does not just run things according to the laws of nature, but continually puts forth His will into existence (*Havayah* means existence, being). This manifestation of *Hashem* was not shown to the forefathers. Thus, *Hashem* was giving Moshe and the people a consolation, in fact *the* consolation: you and the people have earned the higher, continual presence of *Hashem*.

The *Gemara* tells us:[124]

> Rabbi Shimon bar Yochai said, "Come and see how loved are Yisroel. In all the places that the Jews went into exile — in Egypt . . . Babylon . . . Edom — the *Sh'chinah* went with them. How do we know that after they will be redeemed the *Sh'chinah* is also going to be redeemed? Because the verse teaches: *Vishov Hashem ess shivooschoh*, "*Hashem* will return with your returning."

The *Sh'chinah* literally means "Presence." It refers to

the feeling one has that *Hashem* is present. The end of the *Gemara's* statement, though, seems superfluous. If the *Sh'chinah* is with the Jews in exile, then why do we have to be informed that It will be redeemed with them? Can one ever seriously entertain the possibility that It will be left behind?

One answer is that a person could come to think that the *Sh'chinah* will no longer be with the Jews at the end of their exile because they will be so engulfed in darkness. However, the *Sh'chinah* will never depart. It will remain with the Jews until the very end when they are redeemed, Rabbi Shimon bar Yochai teaches.

The Maharal[125] supplies a deeper answer, an answer based on the idea that it is the very helplessness of exile which deepens our feeling of *Hashem*'s presence. Our continued existence in an exile state goes completely against the laws of nature. When we realize that we are alive only because of *Hashem*'s special intervention, His help behind the scenes — and without *Hashem*'s presence, we could not possibly exist — then we feel the *Sh'chinah.* We sense that *Hashem* must be there pulling the strings.

To make the point more personal, the Maharal ties this idea to another *Gemara* which states that when one visits a sick person, he must sit lower than the sick person because "the *Sh'chinah* is over the head of a sick person." A healthy person is independent. He goes about without needing the help of others. Consequently, the

Sh'chinah tends to go unrecognized. However, the sick person requires outside help, and thus is reawakened to the fact that his existence is very much dependent upon *Hashem*. This is what is meant by "the *Sh'chinah* is over the head of a sick person." The sick person has gone from an awareness of *Hashem* as *Kail Shakai*, the *Hashem* who lets 'nature' run its seemingly independent course, to an awareness of *Hashem* as *Havayah*, the *Hashem* who constantly interacts with creation.

That explains the statement that "In all the places that the Jews went into exile . . . the *Sh'chinah* went with them." Exile is a place which cultivates awareness of *Hashem* as *Havayah*. What then does the last statement, that the *Sh'chinah* will be redeemed with the Jews at the final redemption, mean?

One might mistakenly think that the *Sh'chinah* is present only while one is in the midst of suffering pain. Once the pain passes, however, the extra intensity of the presence of the *Sh'chinah* passes as well. If I could compare it, picture yourself in a very dark cave with others. Everything is pitch black. Suddenly, you reach in your pocket and find a small candle. You fumble around for a match, light it, and then light the candle. Despite its size, the tiny candle lights up the entire cave for everyone. Nothing is appreciated more than that little candle. When the group finds its way out of the cave and into the sunshine, the light from the candle, which was once so appreciated, will become totally insignificant.

This is the parable for the *Sh'chinah* which we discover in our suffering, in our darkness; it is like a candle lit in a dark cave. However, the question arises: When we are redeemed — when the brilliant sunshine of redemption banishes the darkness of exile — what significance will this little amount of *Sh'chinah* that we felt during our dark days have? What consolation can we really have, when, in the end, our discovery of the light of the *Sh'chinah* in exile will be like candlelight in the face of sunlight?

To this, Maharal explains that Rabbi Shimon bar Yochai said: "When the time comes for Yisroel to be redeemed from exile, the *Sh'chinah* will be redeemed with them," meaning that the *Sh'chinah* you discover in exile will "be redeemed" (i.e. go along) with *you*; the appreciation you feel now in exile and pain will *not* be drowned out by the great revelation of *Sh'chinah* which will occur at the Redemption. At the time of the Redemption, when life will return to the way it was meant to be, that original *Sh'chinah* revealed during the exile will not disappear.

These are extremely comforting words. Think of it this way: Imagine a mother with twelve children. Every child feels it has a mother. In truth, each child gets only one-twelfth of its mother. However, if one of the children becomes sick, then the mother will give that child more than the normal allotment of attention.

Now, imagine that the child becomes so sick that it has

to be rushed to the hospital. The mother will drop everything and spend twenty-four hours a day by the child's bedside, if need be. While she is tending his every need, the child awakens and suddenly says, "Mother, I always knew that you were my mother. But I never knew that you loved me so much. You are attending me every moment. It was worthwhile to get so sick just to find out what a wonderful mother I have. In fact, perhaps I am better off remaining sick so that I do not lose this special feeling I have for you."

The mother tells the child, "Now that you know to what extent I love you, when we get home and everything returns to normal, you will know that my love for you is just as great."

It is the same way with the Jewish people. Whatever exile we went into, we realized that we could not survive if the *Sh'chinah* was not there with us. When we lost our independence, we realized how much we truly depended upon *Hashem*. When the Redemption comes, however, who says that we will retain this feeling and understanding?

Rabbi Shimon bar Yochai says: "When it comes the time for Yisroel to be redeemed from exile, the *Sh'chinah* [they felt in exile] will be redeemed with them." It is as if *Hashem* says, "When you get well (i.e. when you are finally redeemed in the End of Days) I promise you that you will not lose the feeling of My closeness you experienced during the pain and sickness of your exile.

That feeling will persist with you even after you recover. It is yours forever."

That is what *Hashem* told Moshe. Your forefathers only knew Me as *Kail Shakai*, the *Hashem* who set up and maintains nature. My essential name *Havayah*, however, I did not make known to them. They did not suffer the Egyptian exile. Only now, when you and the Children of Israel are experiencing the worst torment of the Egyptian exile — only now is it possible to know Me by My most intimate and personal name, that I am their *Havayah*, their existence. And from now on, this personal name will be made known to the Children of Israel. They have gained the benefit of suffering. And they will never lose this level.

To take it one final step, the revelation of *Havayah*, first revealed to Moshe, will reach its climax with the coming of *Moshiach*. Our Sages tell us that the *Moshiach* was born on *Tisha B'Av* afternoon.[126] *Tisha B'Av* is the most solemn day in the Jewish calendar, the day when both the First *Bais HaMikdash* and the Second *Bais HaMikdash* were destroyed and burned. *Tisha B'Av* afternoon was actually the height of the burning down of the *Bais HaMikdash*, when all hope was lost.

If your house is burning down, you say to yourself, "Maybe, at least one room will be spared." Then, as the burning continues into the afternoon, it gradually dawns on you that everything is lost. That is the way Jews felt *Tisha B'Av* afternoon. However, it was precisely at that moment, *Chazal* tells us, that *Moshiach* was born.

The same holds true for every individual. Each of us is a microcosm of *Moshiach*; we each harbor within ourselves a point of *Moshiach*. When *Hashem* strips us of everything, including the things which seemingly represent His closeness to us — and there is nothing more symbolic of that closeness than the *Bais HaMikdash* in Jerusalem — it is equated to the birth of *Moshiach*. For when all other supports and symbols are taken away, and there is nothing left except you and *Hashem*, then you are connected to *Hashem* with nothing in between. That uniquely close connection brings forth the point of *Moshiach* within you.

When we rediscover a new closeness to *Hashem* — a new and even greater aspect of ourselves, our *komocha* — then we are, in a way, our own *Moshiach*; we have consoled our loss of the *Bais HaMikdash*, our symbolic closeness to *Hashem*, with the gain of our actual selves. And that gain of self is ours forever.

Thus, when you, dear reader, realize how helpless you are, and you are thereby reminded how dependent on *Hashem* you are — and that you do, indeed, have a close relationship with your Maker every day, every hour, every second — that is the discovery of your own personal *Moshiach*; that is the discovery of the essential name of *Havayah*, the revelation of the *Sh'chinah*.

And that revelation lasts forever. When you think about it, it becomes a source of infinite consolation.

APPENDIX

COMMON QUESTIONS

The following supplement consists of answers to common questions people ask related to the theme of this book. The answers put forth are not all necessarily self-contained. Rather, they may assume some familiarity with the contents of the book. Keep that in mind.

Also, please keep in mind that these questions represent only a smattering of the possible questions one can ask on the subject. If you have a question we have not answered here or in this book, or if you need clarification on any of the answers proffered here or in the book, please write us at Shalheves.

QUESTION 1: No matter how much you rationalize it, I cannot see how a benevolent G-d could possibly allow evil in His world. And you cannot blame mankind's free will for the existence of evil. Why would G-d even allow the possibility of evil? What advantage could there possibly be to evil?

ANSWER: Of course, we cannot and should not presume to analyze *Hashem*'s thinking. Nevertheless, we can understand this on some level.

It is a hard and fast rule: *Hashem* is all-powerful and all-good. He is capable of performing any good for us at any time, and He only wants good for us. However, to just give "good" is not the ultimate good. *The greatest gift one can give another is the wherewithal to stand on his or her own.* In other words, the greatest gift is one which gives the recipient reason to believe that the gift was not a gift (i.e. that it was somehow earned.) That is why jobs are greater than welfare checks. A healthy person wants to earn his bread, and, therefore, there is nothing greater than giving him this ability.

Hashem gave us the ability to earn His goodness. (That is part of His absolute goodness.) If He did not give us the ability to earn His goodness, then the goodness He gave us would not be the ultimate good. We would be little more than automatons doing nothing but receiving goodness.

The mechanism through which *Hashem* gives us the ability to earn His goodness is called free will. Through free will we have the opportunity to go against *Hashem*'s will, to forfeit our goodness. And, therefore, when indeed we do use our free will to follow *Hashem*'s will we truly earn His goodness.

For will to be free, two opposite poles must exist: good and evil. Good is synonymous with *Hashem* and thus always exists, just as it always has and always will.

Evil, on the other hand, is a creation of *Hashem*. It creates the potential known as free will. Therefore, even though it is by definition evil, as *Hashem*'s tool for creating free will it too plays a vital function in the overall good of creation.

Thus, we have the first benefit of evil: it creates the possibility of free will.

There is another benefit we can deduce from *Hashem*'s creation of evil. Free will is the ability to deny our own good — to freely choose bad over good. The real problem with the opportunity to choose bad over good, though, is that after a while it no longer seems bad to us. In fact, it begins to look good. We grow insensitive to bad inside us and around us. We even become convinced that what we are doing, the way we are living, is absolutely good — when in reality it may not be.

The most extreme example of this is the Nazis. Hitler and his cohorts did not think they were evil. Quite the contrary: they thought they were performing the greatest service to mankind by exterminating Jews and other "subhumans" in order to pave the way for the emergence of the "master race." That, unfortunately, was the legacy of Nazi Germany.

We have to realize that all of us are prone to feel that we are good no matter what we do. The real danger in that is: rather than changing our actions to align with true good, we accept evil as a standard and then create a philosophy or a psychology which supports it. (For instance, "That's not stealing, it's free enterprise." Or, "I'm not anti-semitic; I'm a Jew.")

What is the true good? It should be obvious that man alone cannot be the interpreter of good. Only *Hashem* can define it. Otherwise one man's morality is another man's genocide.

In order to prevent a situation where the choice of bad perpetuates itself until the chooser loses all sense of good, *Hashem* built a failsafe into the system — a reminder. That reminder is evil. Evil is a symptom; it is a natural result of using free will to choose bad. Like the physical sensation of pain or pangs of hunger, it signals us that somewhere along the line something is wrong — somewhere we (the individual or we the group) chose bad over good. And then, like pain, that very evil motivates us to seek a cure and rechoose good over bad.

To briefly summarize, then, we have now outlined two purposes of evil. First, the inclination in each of us to choose evil over good is the mechanism of free will. As we said, for will to be free it must be balanced between two opposing forces. The ability to choose good in the face of an equally tempting choice of bad makes the choice of good that much more meaningful.

Second, even when one chooses bad which results in evil, that in itself can be the trigger for rechoosing good. The presence of evil motivates the soul not yet completely numb to good to stand up and resist it. And when one is outraged by evil enough to resist it the evil becomes transformed from a negative force into a positive force. As the *Gemara* teaches: anyone who returns to *Hashem* out of love not only has his sins forgiven but has those sins converted into merits![127] The dynamic operating behind this teaching is that the sins which once distanced the perpetrator from *Hashem* have now become means of attaining a closeness to *Hashem.* The sins become the fuel upon which the fire of love of *Hashem* is kindled.

Therefore, *evil is not a concession. Hashem* can do anything He wants. He created the agency of evil to be very much part of the plan.

Let me explain this idea using the words of *Chazal* (the Sages). After each day of creation (excluding the second day) the Torah tells us that *Hashem* saw that everything He had made was good. After the sixth day, however, the wording is different. It says that *Hashem* saw that everything was *tov meod*, "very good." What on the sixth day led to Him to call it "very good"?"

Chazal tell us that it was the creation of the evil inclination![128]

That seems difficult to understand. However, each of us was created with two inclinations: one for good and one for evil. The good inclination is represented by the word *tov* in this verse, while the evil inclination is represented by the word *meod.* (The word *tov* means "good." The word *meod* means "very." *Tov meod*, the term *Hashem* used at the conclusion of the sixth day of creation, means "very good.")

The lesson is that *the purpose of the inclination for evil is to enhance good — to make it "very good." Tov* only becomes *tov meod* because of the resistance offered by the inclination for evil!

Let me illustrate this.

Imagine a waterhose. If you want the water to reach

far, then two contradictory forces are needed. First, you need a high amount of water pressure. And, second, you need a nozzle which limits the water from exiting. A large supply of water with a large opening will not send the water far; similarly, a very small opening with a small amount of water pressure will not work. Only the combination of high water pressure and a small nozzle will spray the water to a distant spot.

In order for our actions to reach far, two things are needed: a great surge for good and a great resistance to that good.

I have seen this concept borne out again and again. In almost no time, people totally alienated to the standard of good which the Torah talks about became bursting wells of knowledge and character perfection. As *Chazal* say: Even completely righteous people cannot stand in the same place as *baalei teshuva,* people who overcome evil and adversity to return to the path of good.[129] The completely righteous may have a powerful flow, but they do not have the same nozzle. The more restrictive the nozzle, the further the water goes once enough of a surge is mustered.

Thus, the possibility of evil transforms mere *tov* into *tov meod.* When not overcome, the evil multiplies until even the most passive people cannot tolerate it any longer. And then, when it is finally overcome, the revelation and appreciation of good is far superior.

Let me conclude with one last thought. The Hebrew words *adam* (man) and *meod* (which, we said, means "very" and refers to the evil inclination) are spelled with the same letters but in different orders. (*Adam*: *alef, daled, mem; meod*: *mem, alef, daled*.) This intimates that *adam* (mankind) is a battlefield for the war between the good inclination and the *meod,* the evil inclination. In other words, he only earns the title "man" when he wars with his evil inclination.

Evil is part of Hashem's plan of creation. It is there to be overcome. In fact, the conquest and ultimate eradication of evil is the essence of man.

QUESTION 2: Why didn't the great rabbis of prewar Europe tell Jews to leave Europe and emigrate en masse to Israel or America?

ANSWER: You cannot outsmart *Hashem*. This is a basic Torah teaching. The last thing Yosef (Joseph), and our forefather Yaakov wanted, was to go down to the land of Egypt. However, this was *Hashem*'s decree, and the unforeseen string of events behind the sale of Yosef and the family's subsequent descent into Egypt came about despite everyone's great efforts to avoid it. Sometimes, *Hashem* issues a decree and there is no escape.

It goes so far that He will even confuse the mind of the wisest of men, if need be. The *Gemara* teaches us that when the great Rabban Yochanan ben Zakkai came before the Roman general Vespasian and failed to take the opportunity to ask him to spare Jerusalem, that was an example of *Hashem* "twisting the wise man around," (i.e. confusing even the wisest of men). The same can be said about the rabbis in Europe before the Holocaust: When *Hashem* issues a decree, He even takes away the minds of the rabbis. That is part of the decree.

On the other hand, it is possible that some rabbis knew exactly what was going to happen and still chose not to reveal it. The precedent for this is also in the Torah. While Yaakov was suffering over the loss of Yosef, *Chazal* tell us that Yitzchak knew exactly what had happened to Yosef and where he was. Nevertheless, Yitzchak refrained from telling his son Yaakov because he knew the matter had to remain hidden. So, too, we can assume that the inevitable was not hidden from certain great rabbis in prewar Europe, but they knew the matter had to remain hidden.

The great Chofetz Chaim did indeed publicly exhort people to change their ways, numerous forewarning them with visionary insight of the ominous path they were heading down. Rabbi Meir Simcha of Dvinsk wrote in a book posthumously published in 1927: "Those who think Berlin is Jerusalem . . . [will cause a] a howling stormwind will arise [and bring about their destruction]."[130]

Of course, whether they knew or did not know, the truth is that there was no place to run. America had closed its gates to immigrants, and England had even tighter clamps around Palestine. As is well-known, a boat full of escapees from Hitler's Holocaust sought entry into the "free" world and was sent back to Europe. There was no place to run. The rabbis knew that just as everyone else did.

Rather than directing people to emigrate en masse to Palestine, the great rabbis realized that without the people undergoing inner change, no emigration or other action would be able to prevent the inevitable. Let us say that somehow the British and Arabs allowed millions of Jews to settle in Palestine before the war. Rommel (Germany's greatest general) was at the doorstep of Palestine in 1940. The Jews who were already there survived only because of a last minute miracle which led to Rommel's defeat. Nevertheless, had *Hashem* willed it, Jews in Palestine would have been just as vulnerable to extermination at the hands of the Nazis as they were in Europe. Instead of Poles and Europeans energetically helping the Nazis exterminate Jews, we can be sure that the infamous Mufti of Jerusalem would have had little problem inspiring the Arab masses to do the job of genocide at least as well. The bottom line is: You cannot outsmart *Hashem*.

Despite the inevitability of the fate of the Jews of Europe, there was great advantage to seeking out the advice of — and then listening to — the words of the leading Torah sages. If, in the end, one was going to die in a concentration camp or in the forests of Poland or Russia then at least those who listened to the rabbis earned the merit of dying as a result of the advice of *Hashem*'s mouthpiece in this world: the great Torah sage.

QUESTION 3: People denigrate the fact that during the Holocaust Jews went "like sheep to the slaughter." Is it indeed denigrating? Wouldn't it have been better to put up a fight, even if their situation was hopeless?

ANSWER: The only time it is meaningful to put up a fight is when there is a possibility of saving yourself without endangering others. If your situation is hopeless, and by resisting you may cause others to be killed faster, then bravery in that case is to accept your death without fighting.

If, on the other hand, resistance can save lives, then it is an obligation to resist. However, that was not the situation in the Holocaust. The Nazis subdued the vast armies of France, Britain, and Russia. Whenever internal resistance arose in places they controlled, they responded with even greater cruelty. As we said in the previous question, sometimes a situation is irreversibly decreed from Above. The Torah predicts that a time will come when "one of them chases a thousand of you."[131] When *Hashem* issues that decree, no amount of cleverness, military strength, training, organization, or anything else of that nature can make "the thousand" turn around, fight, and win. And this is even more so when the "one" has the power, ruthlessness, and weaponry of the Nazis from 1933 to 1945.

If Jews had to go to their slaughter, then the most dignified way was to go acceptingly. Contrary to what many people think, the Jew who accepted death with peace befuddled and sometimes even outraged the Germans. (See the story about the children in Chapter 5 who danced on *Simchas Torah* as they were led out to the gas chambers.) Through such genuine peaceful acceptance, the German saw the greatness of the Jew, and that unsettled him.

The Torah compares the Jew to a dove. When a chicken is about to be slaughtered, it kicks and shrieks wildly. A dove, on the other hand, stretches forth its neck, and accepts its death with dignity. That is part of its greatness.

For Jews in Nazi-occupied Europe to accept the inevitable with dignity, despite the fact that others might have accused them of being sheep-like, was in itself a radical response. Militant, warrior-like, fight-to-the-death pride was what Hitler was all about. Jews who accepted their fate when there was no other choice resisted what Hitler represented at the very core. And that was the bravest and most heroic response one could have.

QUESTION 4: If, as *Chazal* say, "no prayer returns empty,"[132] (i.e. unanswered) then what happened to all the prayers Jews in Europe prayed before and during the Holocaust? For that matter, what happens to all of our prayers that do not seem to get answered?

ANSWER: Prayer has a peculiar property. Sometimes, you see the result of it immediately. Sometimes, you do not see it until much later. Many of those prayers uttered during the Holocaust are coming into effect now. When you see a completely alienated Jew rediscover his or her heritage, know that it is because that person is a recipient of the prayers of righteous grandparents or great-grandparents in Europe who prayed so fervently for deliverance.[133] (See also Question 6.) No prayer returns empty. Sooner or later it is fulfilled.

This is a key idea applicable to all types of suffering.

Let me illustrate it in regard to the suffering of the childless couple.

Everything good that *Hashem* gives us must be preceded by prayer. Now, imagine a man who has fifteen children and three hundred grandchildren. When he comes before his Maker, he is told that he is given "credit" for three children and thirty grandchildren.

"What about the other twelve children?" he asks.

"You never prayed for them. In fact, you prayed that you would not have them. You even went to seek permission not to have them. Of course, you could not go against My wishes. I had to smuggle those souls into this world despite your wishes. I can give you credit for babysitting, for the price of diapers, etc., however, I cannot give you credit for those children because you never prayed for them. You never wanted them."

Next, a childless couple comes to the world-to-come. All their life, they prayed day and night for *Hashem* to give them children. Yet, *Hashem* never gave them children. Nevertheless, they are informed, "You get credit for 3,000 children and 10,000 grandchildren."

"How could that be?" they ask. "We did not even have one child."

"True. However, there were twelve children from the previous couple who were unwanted. Your prayers earned them for you. In addition to those twelve children, your prayers earned you five from that couple, three from that one, seven from that one, etc."

Prayers are always answered, but somewhere else. In the next world, the *olam haEmes* (the World of Truth), we will know how and where each prayer was answered. Thus, regardless of how hopeless the situation looks, one should never give up and stop praying. Every prayer returns paid-in-full, one way or another, sooner or later.

QUESTION 5: If the destruction of a large portion of Jewry was decreed from Above, why did *Hashem* allow it to happen to European Jewry, the cream of the crop, the center of Torah observance and ideals?

ANSWER: Imagine a person born and raised in the most primitive, jungle society. This person, who had never seen a structure more than one-story high, is brought to a modern city — to downtown Manhattan. Obviously, he will be awestruck. He had never seen anything like a skyscraper. No matter how intelligent he is, he will have no idea how such structures could be built.

As he's gazing in awe, suddenly he sees a twenty-story building — a $50 million, landmark building — demolished by tractors and bulldozers. After they demolish the building, they start digging up its foundation. Twenty feet, thirty feet, forty feet — they dig into the ground. Finally, he cannot contain himself.

"What are they doing?" he asks. "It was such a magnificent structure."

They answer him, "You see the skyscraper next to the building they just demolished? They are going to build a twin tower right next to it."

He starts laughing. "You must be crazy. You think I am primitive? You people are taking a big, expensive building and demolishing it. Why not just build an additional hundred stories on top of the twenty-story building?"

He does not realize, of course, that in order to build a 120-story skyscraper you need a deeper foundation than the one required for a twenty-story building. You explain it to him until he finally understands. He has another question, though. Earlier, he was shown a "bombed-out" section of the East Bronx where property was obviously much cheaper.

"If you people are so smart," he asks, "then why did you have to knock down such an expensive building? If you are going to demolish one building to put up another, then at least do it in the cheaper section where you are not destroying such a costly structure."

No matter how much you try to explain to him the intricacies of real estate value, he will laugh. He will attack you, because he does not have the faintest idea how civilization works. Nevertheless, a sharp businessman knows that wherever the most expensive buildings are getting demolished, that is where the most valuable location is.

None of us have perspective on our lives. We see only a fragment of the picture. We are like the primitive jungle dweller who comes to the city for the first time. Until we begin to inform ourselves and see our lives in the perspective of our people's past and future we disbelieve, ridicule, and deny that which we do not yet have the tools to understand.

Hashem has a design for the world. He knows what He is doing when it comes to fashioning the history and happenings of this temporary world. We can attempt to understand His design as much as is humanly possible; however, the bottom line is that we are not *Hashem*. In *Hashem*'s design, the Torah tells us that the Jewish people are promised eternity. That eternity must be built on a foundation which can support it. Therefore, when you observe that *Hashem* comes and takes one-third of the Jewish people — the backbone, the prime real estate of Israel — demolishing them (in the Holocaust) and digging up their foundation deeper and deeper (in the ensuing spiritual Holocaust), you have to realize that the structure put up in its place will be a super-structure.

Of course, that super-structure is the long prophesied Third *Bais HaMikdash*, the eternal *Bais HaMikdash*; so, too, therefore, the foundation of the Third *Bais HaMikdash* — the people of Israel who populate the Third *Bais HaMikdash* era — must be sufficiently deep in order to support that super-structure.

One of our prayers is worded: ". . . and eternal life He has *planted* in our midst." The process of attaining eternity is likened to the sowing of seeds. When you plant a seed you must first destroy the ground by plowing it up. And then you must throw the tiny seed in, as if throwing it away. And then the ground has to become wet and muddy which causes the seed to decay.

Now, we are aware that the process eventually produces a beautiful plant. However, to the ignorant bystander, each step appears to be the epitome of destruction. Yet, we all know that is a mistaken impression. In the final analysis, the acts of destruction can only be appreciated when one realizes that they are part of a process that occurs over time. They are part of the cycle of rebirth. That is true for seeds as well as for people, both on the communal level and the individual level.

"Sow in tears; harvest in song."[134] The process of sowing seeds is perforce painful. Nevertheless, the pain is in direct proportion to the eventual pleasure. The tears one sheds at sowing time becomes the song one sings at harvest time.

QUESTION 6: I can understand how suffering could have benefits for communal Israel. However, how is it possible to conclude that suffering ultimately benefits each individual sufferer?

ANSWER: The suffering of Jews, especially those in the Holocaust, was not just beneficial to the whole. Each one who suffered benefitted from it. The benefit may not have been immediately apparent. It may not yet even be apparent to us today. However, the suffering of each individual, down to the most minute detail, is calculated from Above.

Let me illustrate this with the story of a Jew who had managed to survive the worst the concentration camps had to offer. Two hours before the Allied soldiers were to liberate the camp, the Nazi commandant convened the Jews. He singled out this one man and told him, "For five years you have survived this camp and never once did you eat non-*kosher* food. I know you have risked so much to keep the smallest details of your religion. However, you were willing to take the risks because you knew you were going to die; your life meant nothing to you. Now, however, you will be freed in two hours. Let's see how much your religion is really worth to you. Here is some pork. Eat it now or I will kill you right here."

Excluding the three cardinal sins of murder, adultery, and idolatry, a Jew is commanded to transgress the Torah to save his life. Nevertheless, when the oppressor's intention is explicitly to get the Jew to deny the Torah, then even if he tells him to change the color of his shoelaces, the Jew must be prepared to give up his life.

So it was with this Jew in the camp. He refused the pork sandwich and was killed for doing so.

Later, when the Jew's daughter found out how her father had forfeited his life just two hours before liberation because he refused to eat pork, her grief was compounded beyond her capacity to bear. Upon settling in the land of Israel, she became irreligious and raised her children to be irreligious like herself.

One of the ways this woman tried to indoctrinate her children was by sending them into Tel-Aviv to buy pork. Her son, a fully secularized non-religious Israeli, was on line to buy pork one day when something strange happened. Waiting on line, pushing for a better position, the story of his grandfather suddenly came to his mind. He stood there thinking, "How can I be here pushing to buy the very food my grandfather gave up his life in order not to eat?"

The young man got off the line, and decided then and there never to eat anything non-*kosher* again. Some time later he decided to keep *Shabbos.* Eventually, he decided to start learning Torah. He excelled at his studies, and now heads one of the most influential organizations for reeducating Jews about Judaism.

Some people, like the Nazis who saw this Jew's grandfather die rather than compromise his religion, perceived the event as a *kiddush Hashem*, a sanctification of *Hashem*'s name. And that sanctification impacted them immediately. However, other people perceived the event as a *chilul Hashem*, a desecration of *Hashem*'s name. The positive seed in the event was not immediately apparent. Now, however, years later, it is possible to look back and see clearly how that Jew's action constituted one of the highest acts of *kiddush Hashem.* His very action was the direct cause of a renewed allegiance to *Hashem* of not only his grandson but many, many, many other Jews of today. That will be rewarded in the next world as great as any act imaginable.

Suffering which does not involve life or death consequences also benefits the sufferer. As is well-known, wealth and ease often destroy people, turning them into self-centered, morally weakened individuals. On the other hand, persevering through and overcoming a serious test of suffering raises a person to moral and spiritual heights. The bottom line is that the positive after-effects of all forms of suffering are precisely calculated to benefit not just the whole nation, but the individual as well.

QUESTION 7: You said (in chapter 6) that even a Jew whose life was anything but holy (the "ram-type" Jew) became holy when he was slaughtered by the Nazis. However, if that is so, then what advantage was there to living a righteous, self-sacrificing life when, in the end, eternity and holiness were essentially guaranteed for all Jews?

ANSWER: We Jews pray that we "should not be embarrassed forever" (i.e. in Eternity). What can make one embarrassed in Eternity? People exist on many differing levels in Eternity, and one's level is determined in life. ("Level," in this instance, means ability to experience the pleasure of *Hashem's* presence.) We pray, therefore, that we should not be embarrassed by our level.

Now, the Jew who was made holy (a *kodosh*) by his slaughter at the hands of the gentile entered Eternity. However, he did so only through the gentile. The righteous (*tzevaos*) Jew, though, attained his holiness on his own, through his own self-sacrifice. Thus, he is not embarrassed; he earned his level on his own. And that accomplishment makes all the difference in the world.

If so, one can counter, then why did *Hashem* let righteous Jews be slaughtered by gentiles? What did the Jew who was already earmarked for a high level in Eternity gain by his slaughter?

The Ari HaKodosh — the holy Ari — said that there is no higher level of closeness to *Hashem* than when one is killed because he is a Jew. Rebbi Akiva and other sages like him looked at their martyrdom as a privilege of the highest order.

Of course, one must keep in mind that Judaism is not a religion of martyrdom; it is a religion of life, a religion which places primary emphasis on living. However, all of us realize that sooner or later we must face death. The question is: What type of death will we face? To this the Ari says that being killed because one is a Jew is the highest level.

Therefore, we must hold on to life as if it is the most precious possession (which it is). And we must sanctify ourselves in life. However, when the time for us to die has arrived, dying like Rebbi Akiva we have to know that that is a privilege. Of course, people may still contend: Rebbi Akiva's death was slow and painful. Couldn't *Hashem* have at least made his martyrdom fast and easy?

As we explained in the book, with every moment that Rebbi Akiva felt the torture of his death, he drew closer to *Hashem*. That closeness (*d'veykus*) more than tempered the physical pain. The Maharam of Rottenberg, who himself died after many years alone in prison, wrote that those who die *ahl kiddush Hashem* (sanctifying *Hashem*'s name) do not feel the sufferings. So, too, great people in the Holocaust remained great; their faces shined and their lips emitted song as they faced death. They did not feel the real brunt of the torture.

In the city of Nitra lived a *gair tzedek*, a righteous convert to Judaism. He had converted about 20 years before the war and raised a Torah family. When the Nazis arrived and started deporting Jews, the gentile parents of this *gair tzedek* said to him, "We have plan for saving you. We will testify that you are a gentile, and you regret ever having been so foolish as to convert to Judaism."

"I am always going to remain a Jew," he answered them.

Eyewitnesses testified that when he was standing in line to the gas chamber, he danced with joy, saying, "*Boruch Hashem*, You gave me the privilege to die because I am a Jew *ahl kiddush Hashem.*"

The truly righteous Jew slaughtered by the Nazis went to his death like Yitzchak, and, like Yitzchak, did so with great *simcha*. They realized the opportunity of their last moment and dedicated their death, as they dedicated their life, to performing *Hashem's* will joy in. (See Question 16 for the story about what originally convinced the *gair tzedek* to convert.)

QUESTION 8: The "ram-type" Jew (Chapter 6) who was slaughtered became holy. However, what happened to the "ram-type" Jew who survived but, in his great pain, ended up totally rejected Torah and Judaism?

ANSWER: That question was asked of the Chasid Yaavetz shortly after the Spanish Inquisition. He answered that those who abandoned Torah and genuinely converted to Christianity were destined to do so anyway. By precipitating their exit with the sufferings of the Inquisition, the Yaavetz wrote, *Hashem* gave them a good excuse for abandoning Torah. This reduced their culpability and thereby created the possibility that their descendants would one day acquire the merit to genuinely return to Torah Judaism.

Applying his answer to the Holocaust, we can perhaps say that the phenomenon of return to Torah by so many young Jews whose parents and grandparents were ardent communists, atheists, and scoffers of Torah is rooted in the fact that *Hashem* gave their parents and grandparents an alibi for their defection. The severity of persecution of the pre-Holocaust and Holocaust eras ultimately worked in their favor regarding their children and grandchildren.

There is a second way to answer the question of the abandonment of Judaism due to suffering. The Zohar says that before *Moshiach* comes, the souls of the *erev rav* (the "mixed multitude" which went out of Egypt with Moses and the Jews) will have to be sifted from the people. Their original conversion to Judaism was laced with questionable, ulterior motives (and they were the ones who led the revolt of the Golden Calf). By the End of Days their souls will be sent into Jewish families with the option to fight to remain Jewish or to leave the fold once and for all.

Of course, no one can know for sure whether a Jew deeply involved in the process of abandoning Torah is from the former group or from the *erev rav*. Nevertheless, even if the Holocaust did indeed trigger the abandonment of Judaism by Jews, we can glean some understanding of why *Hashem* might have designed it.

QUESTION 9: In Chapter 2, you said Avraham's question ("How will I knew that my children will inherit [the Land You promised me]?") was not a mistake revealing lack of faith (and that, consequently, the decree of exile which followed was not a punishment). However, if Avraham's question was not a mistake, what was it?

ANSWER: Imagine a multimillionaire who has a son to whom he wants to bequeath his wealth. He can give him the money as a gift. However, the chances are that the son will not appreciate the money, and will probably squander it irresponsibly. If the father is smart, he will give the son only $100,000, put him in business, and let him make all his own mistakes until he goes bankrupt. Then the father will repeat the procedure until the son learns how to make money on his own. At that point, the father can give him the entire inheritance without fear that the son will abuse it.

Understand Avraham's question as follows. "*Hashem*, you have told me that you will reward my work by giving my children the mission to bring the entire world to ultimate redemption. Nevertheless, by doing so you will deprive my children of the privilege You gave me. You gave me the great privilege of possessing nothing to begin with. That was a privilege because it allowed me to attain everything on my own. However, You are already giving my descendants the merit of having me as their forefather. They are not starting with nothing. "How do I know that they will inherit *me*," (i.e. inherit the personal circumstances of originating from nothing)?"

Hashem responded, "If this is what you want, then I will grant your wish. In order for your children to originate as you did, I will have to send them into "a land not their own for 400 years" where they will be oppressed until they will become dry of all merit. From there they will be able to regain everything on their own like you did." (See also *Days Are Coming*, Part II, subsection, *Avraham and the Four Exiles*.)

QUESTION 10: While Avraham's question may not have shown lack of faith, how can you say the same for Yaakov? The way the *Midrash* you cited (Chapter 2) relates Yaakov's question, it clearly seems to be. How else can we understand: "Now that you (Yaakov) did not believe in Me (*Hashem*)" your children will have to go into exile. Doesn't it sound as if the decree of exile was punishment?

ANSWER: No. The three forefathers, including Yaakov, bequeathed to their descendants all the *tools* necessary to bring the world to its ultimate redemption. However, Yaakov, like Avraham as we explained in the question just above, did not want to bequeath the level of *belief* he had in *Hashem* to his descendants. (The tools — yes, the belief — no.) He, like Avraham, wanted them to attain his level of *belief* in *Hashem* on their own. Thus, the words in the *Midrash* can be understood as follows: *Hashem* responded, "Now that you did not [choose to bequeath your level of] belief in Me" to your descendants, they will go into exile where it will be possible for them to acquire their level of belief through their own efforts.

QUESTION 11: If suffering is so beneficial, shouldn't we ask *Hashem* for more of it?

ANSWER: We should *not* ask. In fact, in each morning's prayers we beseech *Hashem* not to test us. The reason is because we can never be sure whether we will be able to stand up to the test, especially if it is particularly difficult. Therefore, we should not ask for suffering. We should try to prevent it and reduce it once it is upon us.

Suffering, by definition, must hurt us where it hurts most. If someone is so aloof from the world that nothing effects him, then he is not really suffering. That level is best illustrated by Reb Zusia.

Reb Zusia lived a harsh life, even by the standards of poverty-stricken 18th to 19th century Poland. He only had one shirt, was always sick, and had no teeth. One time, a person came to the Maggid of Mezerich, Reb Zusia's teacher, and asked him to explain the statement in the *Gemara* which says that a person is obligated to say a blessing on the bad which happens to him in the same way he says the blessing over the good which happens to him.[135]

In particular, it perplexed the person that Jewish law calls for both types of blessings to be said with equal *simcha* — joy. In other words, if you win the lottery, then you say a blessing thanking *Hashem.* However, if you make an investment and lose ten million dollars, you also have to say the blessing "*Baruch Dayan Emes*" — blessed is the True Judge — with the same amount of joy you would have if you were saying the blessing over winning the lottery! This person asked the Maggid how that could be. He could understand the law requiring one to say the blessing, but how was it possible to say it with the same joyful heart?

The Maggid told him to ask the question to his

shammas, his attendant, who at that time was Reb Zusia. After this person came and posed the question, Reb Zusia looked at him with surprise.

"You must have the wrong person."

"You're Zusia, the *shammas,* right?"

"Yes."

"The Maggid said you could answer the question concerning how one can say the blessing over bad events with the same joy as a blessing over good ones."

"Then, you surely have the wrong person."

"Why?"

"Because I never understood that statement either. You see, nothing bad has ever happened to me."

This was the same Reb Zusia who had no money, no clothes, and no teeth. Yet, he could say with a full heart that nothing bad ever happened to him because he was above the happenings of this world. For almost everyone else, Reb Zusia's tests would have been unbearable. Reb Zusia had worked on himself, though, to the point that he honestly was perplexed how anything could be bad.

We are not Reb Zusia, and should not assume so. We are part of the world and are going to be effected by it. Therefore, we should not ask for suffering. However, if *Hashem* sends us suffering, we must be appreciate the fact that he has trusted us with a true life's challenge that can lead to greatness. In our hearts, we have to say, "Hashem, I appreciate the fact that you trusted me enough to give me this challenge. I know that nothing You do is in vain. Suffering is a special opportunity to become great, and if I have been given the test, then I must realize it is a test I can handle because You never give anyone a test which he or she cannot handle."

There is no greater *kiddush Hashem* than a person who takes his suffering and challenges well. That person is translating the abstract principles of Torah into everyday living. The ability to withstand that challenge is a privilege one must work toward. Until *Hashem* deems us up to the challenge, it is our responsibility to react as a normal human being would react and seek to reduce or avoid altogether the pangs of suffering.

QUESTION 12: When tragedy strikes (such as the loss of a dear family member), one is immediately required to say the blessing "Blessed is the True Judge" (*Boruch Dayan Emes*), and to say that blessing with the same joy as if one has just heard good news.[136] Practically speaking, how can the average person truly live up to that and say the blessing over the bad with the same joy as the blessing over good?

ANSWER: The truth is that the blessing *Boruch Dayan Emes* said immediately upon news of the loss can (and should) stay with one the rest of his or her life. In other words, three months later, six months later, a year later, three years later, etc., whenever you feel the pang of the loss, you sigh but should still have the presence of mind to say *Boruch Dayan Emes* (without explicitly saying *Hashem's* name) — it is all for the ultimate good, it is all part of *Hashem*'s plan. One day, as you move further and further away from the tragedy, you will more easily be able to see the kindness of *Hashem* in the act. And when you do, it is then that you are obligated to say the blessing with complete joy.

Each of us has to continually grow and strive to attain new understanding. Therefore, even if at the moment of receiving news of tragedy we could not say the blessing with joy (and *Chazal* tell us that while one is in pain he cannot be held fully responsible for his actions), one day, when we are more removed from the immediate pain and reflect back upon it, we hopefully will be able to do so.

QUESTION 13: Doesn't the philosophy of accepting suffering with love lead to more suffering because the sufferer learns to passively accept suffering rather than learning how to fight to get beyond it?

ANSWER: No. No one suffers more than the amount decreed by *Hashem*. A person has a religious obligation to seek to avoid suffering, and then try to get out of it once it comes upon him or her. However, if there is no way out, then the art of learning how to accept suffering with love is the solution to suffering. And that entails a proper, healthy mental outlook, as we have endeavored to teach throughout this entire book.

Accepting suffering with love is not a passive endeavor. One has to constantly grow and work on oneself to truly feel that the suffering is a blessing from heaven. Imagine a woman who has not been able to have children for fifteen years. Suddenly, she becomes pregnant. The most joyful experience for her is the labor pains. Even though it hurts, she knows that it means she is about to finally give birth to her own child. That fact blocks out the pain, and even makes it something she accepts joyfully.

Not only giving birth, but everything is dependent upon a proper frame of mind. Working to develop that mind-set should not lead to passivity. On the contrary, just as the Torah teaches one to be active in working to develop that frame of mind, so, too, it teaches one to be active in carrying out all the necessary *hishtadlus* (effort)[137] to prevent or alleviate suffering.

QUESTION 14: Can a Holocaust happen again? in America? Why or why not?

ANSWER: Of course, we are not prophets. However, the prophecies of our prophets were meant to be a map for us. And if we read the map right, we can perhaps venture to say the following: There is no point in *Hashem* bringing another Holocaust. The Holocaust put a brake on the mass defection of Jews from Torah which was occurring at an ever-increasing pace in the century prior to the rise of Hitler. Even though observant Jews are now in the minority, the momentum has shifted. An influx of genuine returnees has ensued. That is the result of the Holocaust. And as long as the shift continues, the purpose of another Holocaust ceases to exist.

Of course, the threat of another Holocaust or the like may be necessary to quicken the process. And certainly no gentile nation (including America) is beyond becoming a breeding ground for a new Hitler, G-d forbid. Nevertheless, as long as the momentum continues in the direction it has been going, then we have genuine cause for hope that the Holocaust will not repeat itself. As we said in the book, the choice is holocaust or *teshuva*. The way I read the map, we are past the darkest hour and need only to wake up to the fact that daylight is dawning upon us. (See *Days Are Coming*.)

QUESTION 15: Why are we hated?

ANSWER: We have addressed this question in this book (Chapter 5) and in *Choose Life!* (Part I, Chapter 5, subsection, *The Root of Anti-Semitism*) and will not fully elaborate upon it here. The simple answer is: Esav hates Yaakov. The non-Jew hates the Jew. There is no ultimate rationale. It is a law of nature.

It is a useless venture to try to pin the cause of anti-semitism on some social factor. Nineteenth century Jewish thinking believed that the Jew was hated because he was different. That is why the nineteenth-century Jew pursued assimilation. Not only was his "this-worldly" life no better for it (the Nazis made sure of that), but in the long run he also lost his identity, his identification as a Jew put in this world by *Hashem* to uphold Torah. Today, people espouse other causes and effects. However, the attempt is futile and can only lead to confusion.

If one must have an answer, he must seek the words of *Chazal* who say that Sinai (as in Mount Sinai) is related to *sinah*, "hatred," because at Mount Sinai *Hashem* chose the Jewish people to be His representatives in this world to keep Torah. Although the non-Jew can always convert, it is much easier to hate.

In either event, our chore is to remain true to who we are and true to our mission. It is not for us to worry about how the gentile will react to that.

QUESTION 16: What is the best way to fight anti-semitism?

ANSWER: To behave as a Jew. To be a role model. To be a "light unto the nations."[138] Militancy and responding to every possible act of anti-semitism will not work in the end. Although there may be a time to speak out and even fight, blanket militancy and reactionism are inventions of the gentile mind.

True Jewish militancy should be aimed against the human inclination to deny the presence of *Hashem*. We are in an exile state not by decree of the nations, but by decree of *Hashem*. Antagonizing non-Jews is not beneficial. It is not them to whom we must answer. Even as we live amongst them, we must realize that it is *Hashem* who has given them influence over us, and has done so for a reason.

If the situation seems fearful to us, then we must first turn to *Hashem* for guidance and deliverance. Focusing on the gentile is like lashing back at the stick that strikes you when you should be paying attention to the one who holds the stick. A dog lashes at the stick as if it were the real problem. A human being seeks to appease the one who holds the stick. And in this case, the One who holds the stick really wants nothing more than our attention, not to actually hurt us.

In Nitra, Czechoslovakia, a *gair tzedek* (righteous convert to Judaism) lived. (See the end of Question 7.)

What caused this *gair tzedek* to convert in the first place, right after the first World War, during some of the darkest days for Jews? He would tell people, "Once, passing by a shul on *motzi* Yom Kippur, at the conclusion of Yom Kippur, I saw the faces of my Jewish friends whom I had business dealings with during the year. They radiated something other-worldly and appeared to me as angels. I could hardly recognize them. I said to myself, 'If such a religion exists which can transform simple working people into angels, then I want to belong to that religion.'"

The role of a Jew is to represent *Hashem* in a way that makes the whole world desire to turn back to Him. Nothing, perhaps, does that greater than when the gentile sees simple, ordinary Jews, with whom they have interacted with in mundane settings, behave as a Jew. When a Jew serves as a role model of devotion to *Hashem* and Torah, there is no greater deterrent to anti-semitism. (See the references mentioned at the beginning of the previous question for more on the subject.)

QUESTION 17: You lumped together the early reform Jews with those Jews who completely abandoned Judaism (Chapter 6). Those reform Jews may have been misguided, but at least they claimed some association with Judaism. Is it fair to equate them with atheists, apostates, and outright deniers?

ANSWER: There are two types of money thieves: one who steals and one who counterfeits. The severity of the crime of the thief who steals is measured by *how much* money he stole. One who steals ten dollars is a thief, but will not be punished as much as one who steals $10,000. The more he steals, the greater the punishment.

The severity of the crime of the counterfeiter, on the other hand, is judged on *how well* he printed the phoney money. One who does a poor job copying a $100 bill has committed a crime. Nevertheless, the crime does not really damage anyone, because it is easily recognizable that the bill is a counterfeit. However, one who makes a perfect counterfeit bill, even if only of a one-dollar bill, is a threat to the entire economy, because no one can tell that his bill is a fraud.

One who steals money does not damage the money per se. He just moved it from one domain to another, from its rightful owner to himself. The punishment is dependent upon how much he moved from one domain to the other. The one who counterfeits, however, threatens to undermine the entire stability of the national treasury. He does damage to the actual money. Therefore, how well he printed the money, rather than how much money he printed, is significant in determining the severity of the sentence against him.

Similarly, there are two types of deniers: the non-believer and the "believer." The non-believer denies *Hashem*. He steals from *Hashem*; he takes credit for everything. He cannot see how *Hashem* runs the world, and, indeed, his own life. The more he denies *Hashem*, the more credit he steals for himself. And, therefore, the more of a thief he is.

The deceiver who claims to be a "believer," though,

in some ways can be an even bigger thief. He presents himself as authentic. He claims to be speaking in the name of truth. However, he may be further away than anyone else. He is the counterfeiter. His crime is judged not on how much he denies *Hashem* — because he does not claim to be denying *Hashem* — but rather on how similar the replica he is trying to pass off as authentic is.

Living the Torah is not always the easiest thing, especially for someone raised in a secular and/or non-Jewish environment. It requires work, sacrifice and absorption. Yet, rather than telling the people, "Look, this is the way *Hashem* wants us to live; there are benefits not only in the next world, but in this world as well; you just have to take it one step at a time and accustom yourself to growing into a fuller and more fulfilling observance of Torah" — instead of saying something like that, the Reformers sold their flock a counterfeit bill.

They said, "Look, we are teaching you the real Judaism. All these centuries, your fathers and grandfathers had been living a lie. We, together with the great German people, will make a better world, and adhere to a higher ethical standard, a more authentic truth."

The more authentic-looking the counterfeit, though, the greater the crime. The biggest lie is to deny the words of the Torah and call your interpretation of it "Judaism." Hitler himself had said, "The bigger the lie, the more the people will believe it." Maybe *Hashem* put those words into his mouth because only someone like him could once and for all put to rest the claims of the early Reformers who promoted the biggest lie of all: that high German culture and ethics are a far improvement over the crude, outdated religion of the Torah.

Of course, the Jew who claims to be "Orthodox" and even dresses the part, but who is a liar and a cheat, or who is assimilated at heart, is a counterfeit as well. (Almost all of us have lapses and relatively minor inconsistencies, however, the "Orthodox" counterfeit is the one who is more than casually devoted to his underhandedness or "permissible" assimilation.) Nevertheless, although there have always been counterfeit individual Jews, counterfeit Judaism is a relatively new thing. Until just less than two centuries ago, the Jewish world adhered to the truths found only in Torah. True, there had always been non-observant or counterfeit individuals, however, there were not dominant groups who sanctioned non-observance, and who relegated the Torah to the status of little more than inspired poetry.

Non-observance of Torah is one thing. Making a new form of Judaism which institutionalizes it is another. And then, calling it "Judaism" is nothing but a counterfeit bill of goods.

QUESTION 18: What hope is there for unity among Jews? Is there a solution? Doesn't clinging firmly to Torah principles only further alienate non-observant Jews?

ANSWER: Generally, people unify when faced with a common enemy. The Torah tells us that all Jews have a common enemy. In fact, the battle against this enemy has a name: it is called *mechias Amalek*, the wiping out of Amalek. More than a physical enemy, Amalek is best thought of as a conceptual enemy.

Amalek is the attempt — in whatever way, shape, or form — to get the Jew to deny his identity, or, as we discussed it in Chapter 7, to get the Jew to deny his *komocha*. The source of all Jewish problems is a lack of identity. The less a Jew can answer: Who am I? the more Amalek is winning.

Even a Jew who is Torah-observant can be a victim of Amalek. If he does not see that all Jews are representatives of *Hashem* on a mission to change the world-as-it-is into the world-to-come, then he will not realize how dependent he is on other Jews. He will cling to his group blindly when he could be contributing (in his own way) to a greater unit. The less the Jewish people appreciate the truth of Jewish self and identity, the greater the fragmentation, and, ultimately, the greater the suffering. The more genuine knowledge there is about *Hashem*, Torah, and Yisroel the more unity there will be. (See Chapter 7 for more.)

GLOSSARY

AKEIDA: Literally, “binding,” used in reference to the biblical episode of the binding of Isaac.

AVRAHAM: Abraham.

BAAL TESHUVA: A person who deepens his commitment to Judaism, usually through a “return“ to complete *mitzvah* observance.

BAIS HAMIKDASH: The Temple in Jerusalem.

BAMIDBAR: The fourth of the five books of Moses; literally, “the Desert.’

BERAISHIS: The Book of Genesis; alternatively: Creation itself.

CHACHAM: Wise man.

CHACHMAH: Wisdom.

CHAZAL: The Sages; literally, the first Hebrew letters of the words, “The Sages, may their memory be a blessing.’

CHOMETZ: Leaven, which is forbidden to be eaten during Passover.

CHUPAH: The wedding canopy. Also used as reference to the wedding itself.

CHUTZPAH: Audacity, gall.

DEVARIM: The Book of Deuteronomy.

ERUV: A halachic fence in which Torah law permits Jews to freely carry objects on *Shabbos*.

ESAV: Esau, the twin brother of Yaakov; the son of Yitzchak and Rivka (Rebecca).

GEHINNOM: Term for the Jewish concept of hell.

GEMARA: The Talmud. The Talmud is the oral law transmitted first by *Hashem* to Moses at Mount Sinai and then down through the generations until persecution warranted its being written in the form of the *Mishnah*, and then later on in the form of the Talmud as we have it today.

HAGADAH: The text recited at the Passover meal.

HALACHA (HALACHOS pl.): Jewish law.

HASHEM: G-d; literally, “The Name.“

HASHKAFA: (Torah) outlook.

KABBOLAS (HA)TORAH: The receiving of Torah.

KASHRUS: The laws of keeping *kosher;* see *kosher.*

KIDDUSH HASHEM: Sanctification of *Hashem*’s name.

KIDDUSHIN: The official engagement (with legally binding ramifications) between a couple.

KODOSH (KODOSHIM pl.): A "holy," as used in reference to a martyred Jew.

KOLEL: An yeshiva for advanced studies designed to support full-time learners and their families.

KOSHER: Dietary laws of the Torah; alternatively, "fit," or "proper.'

LUCHOS: The "tablets" of the ten commandments.

MATAN TORAH: The giving of Torah.

MATZAH: Unleavened bread eaten on Passover.

MIDRASH (MIDRASHIM pl.): Repository of the (originally) oral homiletical interpretations of Torah whose primary focus is the moral, ethical principles and teachings of Judaism.

MISHNAH: The pithy statements of Jewish law upon which the discussions in the *Gemara* are centered.

MITZVAH (MITZVOS pl.): A commandment. The written Torah enumerates 613.

MOSHE: Moses.

MOSHIACH: *Moshiach*.

NISUIN: The final stage in the marriage ceremony.

NOVI: A prophet.

PEYOS: Sidecurls.

REBBI: A rabbi, mentor, teacher.

ROSH (PL. ROSHEI) YESHIVA: The head(s) of a yeshiva.

SANHEDRIN: A Jewish court, most notably the Great Sanhedrin of 71 Sages which sat in the Court of Hewn Stones in the *Bais HaMikdash* Mount and served as the Legislative and Judicial branches of the Jewish government.

SHABBOS: The Sabbath.

SHMOS: Literally, "The Names" and referring to the second of the five books of Moses, the Book of Exodus.

SHULCHAN ARUCH: The authoritative code book of Jewish law.

SHIR HASHIRIM: The Song of Songs written by Shlomo HaMelech.

SHLOMO HAMELECH: King Solomon.

SHUL: Synagogue.

SIDDUR: Prayer book.

SIMCHAS TORAH: Festival signifying the completion of the annual cycle of reading the Five Books of Moses, and characterized by joyful singing and dancing with Torah scrolls.

T'FILLIN: The black leather straps and boxes which the Torah commands Jewish men to wear.

TEHILLIM: Psalms.

TESHUVA: Repentance; more literally, "return," and signifying a return to the ways of Torah. See also *Baal Teshuva.*

TISHA B'AV: The Ninth of Av (the Hebrew month which usually coincides with the latter half of the summer). On the ninth of Av, Jews mourn over the destruction of the first and second *Bais HaMikdash* which were both destroyed on the same date 490 years apart.

TORAH: Scripture (the written Torah) and *Gemara* (the oral Torah) comprising the basic source and essence of Judaism.

TZEVAOS: Soldier or host. Used in this book as reference to one who faithfully represents *Hashem* in this world.

VORT: The pre-engagement festivities which signify the first step in a couple's plans to marry.

YAAKOV: Jacob.

YAHRZHEIT : Anniversary of a deceased.

YESHIVA: A school for teaching Torah.

YIMOS HAMOSHIACH: "The days (i.e. era) of the Messiah." As used in this book, it usually refers to the especially difficult times the Jewish people have had to suffer in awaiting the advent of the *Moshiach* and the Messianic Age he will usher in.

YITZCHAK: Isaac.

YOM TOV: Jewish holiday; festival.

YOREH DEAH: One of the four sections of the *Shulchan Aruch.*

ZOHAR: One of the primary sourcebooks of Jewish mysticism, attributed to Rabbi Shimon bar Yochai (c. 120 C.E.).

Z'TL: Abbreviation for *zaicher tzaddik l'brochah* — the remembrance of a righteous person is a blessing.

REFERENCES

1. *Avos* 4:1.
2. *Mishlei* 1:20.
3. The Belzer Rebbi *zt'l*, himself a survivor, said, "If anyone survived, it was only because two *malachim* stood guard over him without break twenty-four hours a day."
4. Rabbi Weissmandel's miraculous escape, his work to save his brethren, his ultimate survival and his resettlement in America is documented in The Unheaded Cry, by ArtScroll/Mesorah Publications.
5. *Mishlei* 9:9.
6. *Sanhedrin* 97a.
7. See also, Part II of *Choose Life!*
8. *Beraishis* (Genesis) 3:19.
9. *Tehillim* 126:5.
10. *Igros* Rabbi Moshe Chaim Luzzatto.
11. *Beraishis* 15:7-21.
12. As explained and elaborated upon in Part II of *Days Are Coming*, by the author, the Jewish people have experienced four major exiles. Exile in this sense does not only mean physical removal from their land; it can mean living under the dominion or influence of a foreign country while in the land of Israel. Such was the case with the Greek 'exile,' the freedom from which is celebrated during Chanukah. In that case, Jews lived in the land of Israel but were threatened more with the spiritual oppression of Greek hellenization than actual physical oppression or exile. By contrast, the first exile, the Babylonian exile, saw the Jews carried off to the land of Babylon by Nebuchadnezzar.
13. *Beraishis Rabbah* 44:15. The symbolism of the four animals as representatives of the four exiles is elaborated upon in Part II of *Days Are Coming*.
14. *Beraishis* 15:6.
15. *Beraishis Rabbah* 44:21.
16. *Beraishis* 28:12.
17. *Vayikra Rabbah* 29:1.

18. Edom is the same as Rome, which became the embodiment of Christianity which grew into Medieval and post-Renaissance Europe which has become Western Society. See *Days Are Coming*, Part II.
19. Ohr HaChaim, *Bamidbar* 20:8.
20. Iyun Yaakov, *Berachos* 32b.
21. *Berachos* 31b et al. See also Maimonides *Yesodei HaTorah* 1:8-12; *Chovos HaLevavos, Shaar HaYichud*, ch. 10.
22. Malachi 1:2-3.
23. As for why G-d loves Israel with a special love, see *Choose Life!*, Part I, Chapter 5, *Who is a Jew?*
24. *Devarim* 14:1.
25. Hosea 2:1.
26. *Shmos* (Exodus) 4:22.
27. Cf. Daas Tevunos 129 (Friedland Edition).
28. Hosea 2:18,21.
29. Jeremiah 2:2.
30. *Baba Basra* 12a.
31. *Aggados HaShas* ibid.
32. See *Choose Life!*, chapter 2, subsection *The Challenge of Sinai.*
33. *Mechilta, Parshas Beshalach.*
34. *Devarim* 34:10.
35. *Asara Maamoros* by R'ma M'Pano (cited in *Seder HaDoros*); *Yuchasin.*
36. *Menachos* 29b. See ahead in Chapter 7, *Rebbi Akiva.*
37. See Appendix to *Choose Life!*
38. For instance, the 1981 assassination of Egyptian President Anwar Sadat, including the name of the chief assassin, the date, Sadat's name and the Hebrew words for president, shot, gunfire, murder, and parade (Sadat was shot and killed during a parade) were all found in a single passage. Similar findings for such events as the French Revolution, the Holocaust, and even the Gulf War have been discovered. Codes research with computers has been going on for only about ten years, yet already it has won the approbation of leading scholars at Harvard, Yale, and Hebrew University. In the letter of approbation to the book *Maymad HaNosaf* (The Added Dimension) mathematicians like Professor Kazhdan of Harvard, who have reviewed the codes research, call the work "serious research carried out by serious investigators." See the article *Back To The Future* reprinted in the Appendix to

Choose Life! for more on the subject.
39. George Wald, Scientific American, Vol. 191 No. 4 (1954) pg. 46 cited in Pathways To Torah, Arachim.
40. *Zohar Beraishis* 117a.
41. Isaiah 11:9.
42. *Hilchos Teshuva* 10:6.
43. "He acquired himself through ten tests, just as the world was built with ten statements." (Maharal, *Derech HaChaim, Avos* 5:2,3)
44. Cf. *Ohev Yisroel* by the Opter Rav.
45. Ramban, *Beraishis* 21:1.
46. *Tehillim* 92:8.
47. See *To Become One* (Chapter 3) by the author.
48. Ibid. Chapter 2.
49. See *Choose Life!*, especially Part I, chapter 5, *Who Is A Jew?*
50. *Shabbos* 88a.
51. Morning prayers.
52. Ibid.
53. *Shmos* 24:7.
54. *Tanchuma, Parshas Noach* 3.
55. *Shabbos* 88a.
56. *Tiferes Yisroel*, chapter 32.
57. *Shmos* 15:2.
58. *Sota* 30b.
59. *Avos* 5:5.
60. See *Days Are Coming*, Part II.
61. *Devarim* 31:18.
62. *Devarim* 31:17.
63. *Shir HaShirim* 1:5. Rashi explains this statement as that of Israel to G-d. However, the Tzror HaMor explains it as we have, as the statement of G-d to Israel.
64. *Michah* 7:15.
65. *Shmos* 15:2.
66. *Divrei HaYamim* I 17:21.
67. *Shulchan Aruch, Orach Chaim*, 65:3.
68. *Shabbos* 89a.
69. *Daas Tevunos* 130 (Friedland Edition)
70. Of course, even though, 'All Israel have a portion in the world to come. . .' individuals under certain circumstances can forfeit that. See further, *Sanhedrin* 90a.
71. *Talmud Yerushalmi, Taanis*.

72. Genesis 1:26. See *To Become One*, by the author, Chapter 2.
73. *Chagigah* 15a.
74. *Shmos* 34:1.
75. *Devarim* 32:4.
76. Jacob and Esav were twins, similar on the outside, yet worlds apart on the inside. For instance, Jacob sat in tents, and contented himself with true spirituality (Genesis 25:27); Esav was a hunter, accustomed to spilling blood and taking what he wanted (ibid.). Esav scoffed his birthright and was willing to sell it for a bowl of lentils (Genesis 25:33,34). Jacob was recognizable through his voice, a quality of spirituality and inwardness, while Esav was known for his hands, the organs of manipulation (*Beraishis* 27:22).
77. See *Choose Life!*, chapter 5.
78. Ibid. Jacob capped the achievements of the forefathers, and therefore only his seed became the full recipients of the effort of all the forefathers. Abraham had an Ishmael, while Isaac had an Esau. These were like the chaff of the Abraham's and Isaac's beings, respectively. Only Jacob, who capped off the spiritual efforts of his father and grandfather with his own spiritual perfection, had offspring who were all considered righteous. (G-d could have only designated Jacob's children to be the tribes of Israel if, in the final analysis, they were all righteous themselves.) Therefore, G-d's promise to Abraham and Isaac became manifest only in Jacob.
79. See the Mark Twain quote cited in *Choose Life!* Part I, chapter 5.
80. *Baba Metziah* 59b.
81. *Devarim* 30:12.
82. See *Choose Life!* Especially the supplemental essay on *Rosh HaShannah.*
83. See *Choose Life!*, especially the supplemental essay on *Rosh HaShannah*.
84. *Beraishis Rabbah* 34:9.
85. Daniel, Chapter 3.
86. *Aitz Yosef* loc. cit.
87. See Chapter 3, subsection *Influx of Knowledge in the Modern Age*.
88. Thirty-one is highly significant because the a person who speaks *loshon hara* (evil speech) potentially transgresses thirty-one Torah prohibitions. *Loshon hara*, literally, 'the evil

tongue,' was the sin of the primal snake in the Garden of Eden. It used its tongue to bring about sin, destruction, and death to the world. As is well-known, Hitler's one real talent was his ability to persuade others through speech. He was a fiery orator who induced an entire continent to sin grievously and bring about destruction and death. In all likelihood, probably only the primal snake, who induced all of mankind extant in his day to sin grievously, can be said to have been more destructive.

89. *Beraishis Rabbah* 56:5.
90. *Kiddushin* 40a.
91. *Shmos* 4:22.
92. *Midrash Tehillim* 90; Rashi, *Shabbos* 88b; cf. *Anaf Yosef* ibid.
93. See Appendix: Questions and Answers.
94. *Hilchos Avodah Zarah* 1.
95. *Ashel,* 'tree' in Hebrew, is spelled *alef, shin, lamed*. These letters stand for *achilah, shisa, lina* — eating, drinking, lodging.
96. *Chagigah* 12a.
97. *Beraishis* 25:5.
98. *Beraishis* 28:4.
99. *Beraishis* 32:29, 35:10.
100. Rashi citing *Beraishis Rabbah*.
101. *Kesubos* 111a.
102. *Beraishis* 25:26.
103. 1760-1832. Most famous for his commentary on *Yoreh Deah* entitled *Chavas Daas*, his commentary on Shir HaShirim is entitled *Tzror HaMor*. Rabbi Tauber has a ten-tape series on Shir HaShirim with the commentary of the *Tzror HaMor*. See the tape list in the back of this book for information.
104. *Sanhedrin* 97b.
105. See *Choose Life!*, especially Part I, Chapter 5.
106. See *Days Are Coming*.
107. *Beraishis Rabbah* 1:1.
108. Chapter 3.
109. *Avos D'Rabi Nosson* 6.
110. *Menachos* 29b.
111. *Megallas Amukos* 186.
112. *Makkos* 24a.
113. *Chagigah* 12a.
114. *Tzidkus HaTzaddik* 95.
115. *Beraishis* 6:12.

116. *Shabbos* 31a.
117. *Sanhedrin* 10:1.
118. *Avos* 1:12.
119. See *Choose Life!*, the Outline of Topics, and Part I, Chapter 5, sub-section *Israel.*
120. Siddur
121. *Devarim* 4:6.
122. See end of chapter 6.
123. *Shmos* 5:23.
124. *Megillah* 29a.
125. *Netzach Yisroel*, chapter 10.
126. *Midrash Eichah* 1:51.
127. *Yoma* 86b.
128. *Beraishis Rabbah* 9:7.
129. *Berachos* 34b, *Sanhedrin* 99a.
130. Meshech Chochmah, *Vayikra* 26:44.
131. *Devarim* 32:30.
132. *Berachos* 32b.
133. See *Choose Life!*, the supplemental essay on Rosh Ha-Shannah, sub-section, *The Power of Kiddush Hashem.*
134. *Tehillim* 126:5.
135. *Berachos* 54a.
136. *Berachos* (54a).
137. See *I Shall Not Want*, chapter 3.
138. Isaiah 42:6.

SHALHEVES

Information and Tape List

SHALHEVES

What is Shalheves?

Shalheves (pronounced Shal-heh-vess) is an organization centered around the efforts of Rabbi Ezriel Tauber. A Torah scholar and businessman, hardly a day goes by without someone coming into his office, seeking his advice on a personal matter.

After years of counseling and lecturing upon request, it became apparent that there were groups of thirsting Jews with special interests who needed regular classes on the topics most relevant to them. Shalheves was started as a network of lectures and classes devoted to groups such as these. Over the years a large tape and video collection accumulated. Even after all this, it was apparent that greater services were needed. That is when the Shalheves (Yarchai Kallah) Seminar Weekend was devised.

What is a Shalheves Seminar Weekend?

It is a gathering of people who want to unplug from the static and noise of everyday life for a few days in order to listen to words of Torah that inspire and challenge.

Who attends Shalheves Seminar Weekends?

Men, women, singles, marrieds, college students, professionals, business people, secular, religious, yeshivish, chassidic, etc. The seminars are of basically two types — one geared for the secular and newly religious, and one geared for the religious.

What happens at a Shalheves Seminar Weekend?

A lot of talking, a lot of eating, some sleeping — all fit around and between a dozen or so power-packed presentations, covering topics like Marriage, The Definition of a Jew, and The Meaning of Shabbos, in addition to ideas like Creation and Its Purpose, Prophecies Materialized in Our Times, and Hidden Codes in the Torah.

Who Speaks at the Shalheves Seminar Weekend?

Rabbi Ezriel Tauber. Rabbi Shimshon Pincus, Rav of Ofakim in Eretz Israel and Rosh Yeshiva of Yeshivas Yerucham. Guest Speakers like Rabbi Shlomo Brevda, Rabbi Yisrael Rokowsky.

For information, contact:

Shalheves
P.O. Box 361
Monsey, N.Y. 10952
(914) 356-3515

The following is a partial listing of tapes in English by Rabbi Ezriel Tauber, including lectures through Winter 1992. We also have a list of tapes in Hebrew and Yiddish, as well as videos. Prices are $3.00 per tape, and $12.00 per video plus shipping and handling. To order or for an updated list contact us at:

Emunah-Torah-Tapes
P.O. Box 361
Monsey, New York 10952
(914) 356-3515

Audio Tapes — BEGINNERS

Number	Title
75	An Introductory Lecture to Non-Commited Jews
93	Business and Torah
146	For Beginners
165 A & B	The Creation and its Purpose
167	Business and Torah
170	Life after Death
176	Is There Everyday Life?
201	Purpose of Life (Part 1)
202	Mysticism in Everyday Life (Part 2)
203	Mysticism in Everyday Life (Part 3)
241	Who Am I?
250	New Times of Teshuva
269	Should We Isolate or Integrate?
295	Real Life
307	Jewish Concept of Woman
316	The Structure of the Jewish Nation
317	To Appreciate Our Role
323	Should We Plan?
338	The Value of Time
394	The Definition of "Yehudi"
757 A & B	Creation and its Purpose
758 A	Definiton of a Jewish Nation
758 B	The Benefit of Suffering
759 A & B	Torah Concept of Marriage
796	Be a Proud Jew
817 A	Torah Concept of Marriage
817 B	Reliance on Effort
818	The Value of Life
855	Lets Represent G-d
872 A	Know G-d
872 B	Our Crucial Days
966 A & B	Secret Codes in the Torah
1003	The Meaning of Happiness
1018	Search for Happiness
1029	Is There Freedom of Choice?

Number	Title
1035	I, As A Representative of G-d
1101	Destiny of Life
1286	The Significance of the Binding of Isaac
1316	Appreciate Life
1341 A & B	Codes in the Torah

Audio Tapes — INTERMEDIATE AND ADVANCED

26	13 Principles of Faith
48	Are You Proud to be a Jew?
50	The Torah Concept of Marriage
72	From the Depths I Call to You
80	Parshas Bereishis
83	The Woman's Torah Leshmo
95	Parshas Vayechi
100	In the Merit of Righteous Women We Were Redeemed
101	A Lecture to Teachers' of Girls
105	Amalek and Pharaoh
108	For a Girl — Leaving Egypt
110	Sefira — in our Time
119	Parshas Yisro — Mishpatim
125	Mourn with Joy
127	Torah Never Went to Golus
132	Mechanics of Teshuva
135	A Real Chesed
136	Teshuva with Simcha
144	The Tree Which is a Fruit
153	Parshas Vayeitsei
161	The Eternal Light
168	Be like Ephraim and Menashah
188	Our Responsibility to the World
192	Make Your Own Luchos
195	Women's Participation in Building the Mishkan
207	Don't Rebel Against the Nations
209	The Four Parshiyos
220	Creation at Matan Torah
232	Bitachon vs. Effort
241	Who am I?
243	Our Share in Moshiach
245	Listen and then Realize
249	Teshuva with Shofar
250	New Time of Teshuva
258 A & B	The Teshuva Prophecy Realized
261	My Only Request of Hashem
266	The Role of Our Mother Rachel
269	Should We Isolate or Integrate?
271	Chanuka 5745
446	Be an Original Jew
517 A & B	The Definition of Truth
518	The Purpose of Creation

Audio Tapes in English — INTERMEDIATE AND ADVANCED

Number	Title
519	Yisroel — Fulfillment of Creation
521	Torah and Tefillah — R. Pincus
523	Effort and Bitachon
524	Marriage of Israel and Hashem
543	Responsibility — Collectively and Individually
544	A Happy Life
546	Kiddush Hashem by Women
552	Enrich Your Life
554	Suffering as Currency
557	Should we be Exposed to the World?
558	The Manna of Today
566	The Golden Calf
569	Building the Bais Hamikdash with Our Fire
600	Meaning of the Akeidah
603	Decoration to G-d
607	Life in Gan Eden
613	The Woman's Role in the Family
618	The Man's Role in the Family
620	"Male and Female He Created Them"
623	The Woman's Role in Judaism
625	A Happy Jewish Family
630	Fashion
632	Multiple Plans in the Universe
635	The Bush Burning in Fire
640	Life with Confidence
646	Shira Before Torah
648	The Jewish Nation's Responsibility to the World
651	Woman's Role in Building the Bais Hamikdash
654	Belief and Knowledge
659	Be Aware of Our Times
661	Split Your Own Sea
666	Benefits of the Jewish Dietary Laws
670	All Israel has a Share in the World to Come
678	Rabbi Akiva's Disciples
682	Let's Do and Listen
688	Thank Hashem for Everything
690	Effort of Competition
691	Stay High — Always
695	Parshas HaMeraglim
704	I, As a Walking Bais Hamikdash
708	Selfless Love
709	Role of a Jewish Girl
711	Fill in Your Time
714	Remember Us For Life
718	Two Ways of Praying
719	Obtaining Love of Hashem
720	Choose Life
722	Take Yom Kippur with You

Audio Tapes in English — INTERMEDIATE AND ADVANCED

Number	Title
737	Love Your Friend as You Love Yourself
740	"Chinuch" — the Real Way
746	Bring Chanukah
752	Love Hashem
753	Discover Yourself
755	Curiosity — Why?
757 A & B	Creation and its Purpose
758 A	Definition of a Jewish Nation
758 B	The Benefit of Suffering
759 A & B	Torah Concept of Marriage
772	An Effective Prayer
777	Fight Amalek
779	Develop Simcha
782	Believing in Hashem
784	Enjoying the Golus
787	To Combat Proudness
789	The Real Simcha
792	The Haman of Today
793	Mordechai and Esther Today
796	Be a Proud Jew
797	Egypt in Our Times
799	The Full Emunah
805	My Share in the World to Come
810	To be High — or Money
817 A & B	Torah Concept of Marriage
819	The Real World
820	Plant Life
821 A & B	The Meaning of Life
822	Crucial Times of Today
823	Our Days of Moshiach
824	The Development of Man
829	The Essence of Torah
832	The First Principle of Belief
833	One Solution for all Problems
836	A Moment of Life
837	I, as a Messenger
838	For Single Parents
840	Live for the Present
843	Let's Build the Third Bais Hamikdash
845	Let's Care for Each Other
845	Discover Your Wisdom
849	Make Use of Your Intellect
851	Questions and Answers
855	Let's Represent G-d
857	The Meaning of Chesed
858	Life as a Service to Hashem
862	Truth
863	Tranquility

Audio Tapes in English — INTERMEDIATE AND ADVANCED

Number	Title
867	What can I Give to Hashem?
869	Let's be Honest
876	Corronate Hashem
878	Make Me King
881	Join Me Totally
883	Do it for Your Name
890	The Meaning of Simcha
893	How Tefillah works
894	The Real Truth
900	Let's Build Om Yisroel
901	Be Aware of Your Duties
902	How is Hashem Telling Me What To Do
903	Definition of Truth and the Essence of Life
904 A & B	Creation and its Purpose
905 A & B	The Torah Concept of Marriage
906	Effort and Bitochon Towards Parnassa
907	Prophecies Materialized in Our Times
909 A & B	Sufferings/Tests During the Times of Moshiach
913	Ner Hashem Nishmas Adam
915	Questions and Answers
920	Why are We Hated?
921	Yaakov's Purchase of Esav's Bechorah
926	Me as Hashem's Candle
927	Money as Eternity
935	Mitzvas Yediah — Emunah
939	Me as a Chanukah Light
943	Veahavta Lereacha Komocha
944	We as Survivors
945	The Meaning of the Image of Hashem
948	Develop the Right Desire
951	Appreciate Your Role
952	Suffering as a Currency
953 A & B	Reliance and Effort
959	Leaving Egypt Today
960	When Children Question Our Values
964	You Cannot Dilute the Truth
966 A & B	Secret Codes in the Torah
967	Prophecies Materialized in Our Times
968	All of Us Have a Purpose
971	How to Generate Simcha
972	Assimilting Whilst Religious
974	Pesach — Purim — Pesach
979	Enthusiasm for Pesach
988	Ahavas Yisroel
993	Yisroel Victorious
995	Carrying Diamonds
977	Every Inch of Life - An Ongoing Bliss to Avodas Hashem
1000	The Value of a Moment

Audio Tapes in English — INTERMEDIATE AND ADVANCED

Number	Title
1003	The Meaning of Happiness
1006 A & B	Chinuch, Courage to say No!
1008	Every Moment A Mission To Hashem
1014	Chinuch for Yourself
1018	Search for Happiness
1019	Build Your Bais HaMikdash
1021	Achievements of Positive Thinking
1023	Turning Sadness into Joy
1028	The Birthday of Moshiach
1029	Is There Freedom of Choice?
1030	The Right Chinuch
1031	Chinuch in T'zneus
1033	The Advantage of Elul
1034	Let's Coronate Hashem
1035	I, As A Representative of G-d
1039	The Concealed Power in You
1048	My Resolution
1055	Power of Prayer
1057	My Role in Creation
1061	The Mitzvah in Teshuva
1070	Days of Moshiach
1073	Positive Speech
1077	Chesed to Yourself
1082	How to Prepare for Our Times
1093	Finding Strength
1094	Getting Things Done
1097	The Definition of Truth
1098	Creation and its Purpose
1099 A & B	The Torah Concept of Marriage
1100 A & B	Golus - the Benefit of Suffering
1102	Depth of Tefillah
1106	Finding Hashem in Business
1107	How to Accept a Loss in the Family
1119	Finding Strength
1120	Sensitivity to Peoples' Needs
1128	Our Crucial days
1129	Our Life as a Plant
1133	How to Wait for Moshiach
1135	Appreciate Being Chosen
1136	Our Times in Depth
1142	Times for Action
1148	Honoring Parents
1149	What are we Really Waiting For?
1153	Waiting for Moshiach
1154	Value of a Moment of Life
1157	My Share in Moshiach
1159	How is Amalek Effecting Us
1169	You as an Artist

Audio Tapes in English — INTERMEDIATE AND ADVANCED

Number	Title
1170	Leaving Egypt Today
1180	Our Crucial Days
1185	Questions and Answers
1186	My Personal Growth
1190	Questions and Answers
1192	We as Rabbi Akiva's Students
1200	The Gift of Torah
1201	My Share in Torah
1209	Harmony in the Home I
1210	Harmony in the Home II
1211	Remembering
1218	How to Grow Every Minute
1221	Today's Bais HaMikdash
1223	Believing
1226	Rebuild the Bais HaMikdash
1228	True Value Vs. Symbolic Value
1230	How to Love a Jew
1233	You as a Bais HaMikdash
1236	How Marriage Helps Us Realize Our Potential
1240	Why Loshon Hara?
1242	The Ultimate Goal
1243	The Real Free Choice
1246	The Man in Nature
1259	Please Corronate Me
1265	A Full Jew
1274	Torah in Business
1280	I, as the Only Man on the Planet
1283	Know Who You Are
1286	Significance of Akeidas Yitzchak
1288	Sarah's Life - All Good
1292	Bitachon in Stressful Situations
1295	The Four Golus
1296	The Meaning of Marriage
1298	Being Thankful
1300	The Benefit of Suffering
1304	The Woman's Role in Marriage
1306	Surprises about Chanukah
1310	Bayomim Hohaim Bizman Hazeh
1315	Appreciate Life
1317	Self Appreciation
1321	How to find a Friend
1322	You come First
1328	"Golus," The Benefit of Suffering
1330	The Meaning of Life
1333	The Greatness of Man
1338	A Time for Renewal
1340	Find Meaning in Life
1359	The Revelation of Israel

SPECIAL TAPE SERIES

Series of lectures for Divorcees
Series of lectures for Childless Couples
Series of lectures for Single Girls
Series of lectures for Widows
Series of lectures for Bereaved Parents

All of the above mentioned tapes are also very helpful for any other kind of problem or difficult situation you might find yourself in.

ADDITIONAL TAPE SERIES (English, Hebrew, Yiddish)

English:
- Chovas Halevavos (100 tapes)
- Maharal - Netzach Yisroel (53 tapes)
- Ramchal - Da'as Tvunos (50 tapes - more upcoming)
- Ramchal - Derech Hashem (7 tapes)
- Ramchal — Mesilas Yeshorim (30 tapes - more upcoming)
- Shir Hashirim with commentary of Tzror HaMor (10 tapes)
- Tanya (52 tapes)
- Series of Tapes for Chassanim (5 tapes)
- Series of Tapes for Kallahs — various women speakers (6 tapes)

Yiddish:
- Chovos Halevavos (51 tapes)
- Tanya (30 tapes)
- Bechol Derochechah Daihu (10 tapes)
- Series of Tapes for Chassanim (5 tapes)
- Ramchal — Mesilas Yeshorim (8 tapes)
- Ramchal — Derech Hashem (12 tapes)
- Maharal — Tiferes Yisroel (52 tapes)
- Maharal — Netzach Yisroel (25 tapes)
- Maharal — Derech Chaim (19 tapes)
- Maharal — Geviros Hashem (14 tapes)
- Maharal — Nesiv HaTorah (9 tapes)

Hebrew:
- Chovos Halevavos (86 tapes)
- Parshas Hashovua (81 tapes)
- Tefillah (30 tapes)
- Ramchal — Mesilas Yeshorim (25 tapes)
- Ramchal — Mamar Haikrim (6 tapes)
- Ramchal — Derech Ez Chaim (7 tapes)

In addition, we have tapes from the complete Seminars in English, Yiddish, and Hebrew. (Series of about 10-12 tapes per Seminar.) Furthermore, we have tapes for Russian-speaking people.

VIDEO-TAPES

1. Hidden Codes in the Torah
2. Prophecies Materialized in Our Times
3. The Definition of Truth
4. Creation and its Purpose
5. Definition of Life
6. Torah Concept of Marriage
7. Harmony and Peace in the Jewish Home
8. "Golus" — the Benefit of Suffering
9. Panel Discussion — Questions and Answers
10. The Significance of Torah and Tefillah
11. The Meaning of Shabbos
12. Times of Moshiach
13. Effort and Bitochon Towards Making a Living
14. Improving
15. Practicality in Day-to-Day Life

כניצול שואה, למד הרב עזריאל טאובר כבר בגיל צעיר על ערכם של החיים. במשך שנים רבות הצליח הרב טאובר לרתק סוגים שונים של קהל מאזינים בכל רחבי העולם ולהשתמש בהבנת החיים המעמיקה שלו, ועם זאת המעשית, כדי לסייע לאחרים לחזק או לגלות מחדש את אהבתם לחיים.

החיים לפניך! הוא ספר המבוסס על שנים רבות של נסיון, לימוד, יעוץ והרצאות של המחבר. זוהי קריאה מעוררת ומלהיבה וחוויה מעשירה, אשר מעל לכל מבליטה ומחזקת את יופים ואת מרכזיותם של החיים.

החיים לפניך!

"החיים והמות נתתי לפניך, הברכה והקללה — ובחרת בחיים! למען תחיה אתה וזרעך" (דברים, ל', י"ט)

- מה הם החיים? מדוע יש לבחור בהם? האמנם מאמין אני באמת שרגע של חיים לא יסולא בפז?
- מהו אושר? האמנם ניתן באמת להשיגו? האם אושר והנאה הן מילים נרדפות?
- מי אני? מה מצפה ה' ממני? מה אני מצפה ממנו?

הדלות האמיתית של העולם בימינו היא שאנשים כה רבים אינם מסוגלים להשיב על שאלות כגון אלו. רבים עוד יותר אינם יודעים מספיק כדי לשאול שאלות. ואין דבר חסר טעם יותר מאשר תשובה ללא שאלה.

משום כך, "**החיים לפניך!**" הוא יותר מאשר ספר של תשובות. הוא מעורר את הסקרנות לשאול שאלות — שאלות הנוגעות בעקרונות היסוד של החיים, עקרונות שמהם נובעים האהבה, האושר וכל הטוב.

החיים לפניך! קיראו אותו! הפיקו ממנו הנאה, צמיחה וגדילה.

בדידות, מבוכה, דומיה - אלו הם התארים אשר, למרבה הצער והאירוניה, נקשרים לעיתים קרובות עם הנישואין, אותם נישואין שנעדו להקל מעל גברים ונשים את המועקות של מצבים אלו. במקום שיהיו מסגרת לשאיפות ולרגשות הנעלים ביותר, הרי ישנם רבים שחיי הנישואין הפכו להיות עבורם בית כלא של כשלון וההזדמנויות שהוחמצו.

- האם יש נישואין חסרי תקוה לחלוטין? כיצד אגיע למימוש ולהגשמה בחיי הנישואין?
- האמנם נמשכים הניגודים זה אל זה? מה ביכלתי לשנות ומה אינו ניתן לשינוי?
- מה היא תכליתם של חיי הנישואין? האם ישנם עקרונות בסיסיים שעליהם מושתתים מאמריהם הרבים של חז״ל בקשר לנישואין?

והיו לאחד הוא דו־שיח הלקוח מן החיים (הדמויות בדויות) של זוג נשוי המחפש תשובות לשאלות אלו ואחרות.

בראשית פרק ב׳ פסוק כ״ד

״על כן יעזב איש את אביו ואת אמו ודבק באשתו והיו לבשר אחד״

פסוק זה צופן בחובו את סוד חיי הנישואין המוצלחים, ואלו המצליחים לחשוף את הסוד - יכולים לשפר את היחסים ביניהם באופן מיידי. למעשה, זוהי הדרך שבה עוזר הרב עזריאל טאובר, מזה שלושים שנה, לזוגות הפונים אליו והשואלים בעצתו. בין דפי הספר עובר כחוט השני דו שיח המכיל את הנוסחה בה השתמש הרב טאובר לטיפול במקרים רבים ולשיקומם של סוגים שונים של חיי נישואים שעלו על שרטון, אפילו כאלו שהיו אומללים למעלה מעשרים שנה!

שיטתו של הרב טאובר פשוטה היא: להסביר את העקרונות המונחים בתשתית האידיאל של התורה כדי לחסן ולחזק את שומעיו לקראת צמיחה ומימוש אישיים של כל אחד מבני הזוג. על ידי הסברת השרשים, הוא מראה לנו כיצד הענפים, הזלזולים והעלים של המצבים האישיים של כל אחד ואחת מאיתנו הם באמת שלמות אחת, שכל חלקיה קשורים זה בזה. כל אלו הופכים את **והיו לאחד** לשילוב מיוחד של המעשי עם המופשט. קיראו אותו. שאבו את מלוא ההנאה ממנו. ומעל לכל - השכילו לגדול ולצמוח בעזרתו.